BARRON'S

NEW JERSEY

GRADE 8

ELA/LITERACY TEST

Tim Hassall, M.A.
President, HASS SAT Test Prep
Cherry Hill, New Jersey

Mary Dillon, Ed.D.
Curriculum Supervisor of English 6–12 and ESL K–12
Hamilton Township School District
Hamilton, New Jersey

About the Authors

Tim Hassall, M.A., is founder and president of HASS SAT Test Prep in Southern New Jersey. He has taught eighth grade English in Voorhees for eighteen years. Tim has written several test prep books, including one other for Barron's, *Barron's NJASK 8 English Language Arts*. He received his Master's from Rutgers with a concentration in creative writing, and he received an Annenberg Fellowship to study at the National Constitution Center.

Mary Dillon, Ed.D., is the curriculum supervisor of English 6–12 and ESL K–12 in the Hamilton Township, New Jersey, school district. Dr. Dillon has attended and presented workshops on Common Core and the PARCC exam, as well as rewritten several curricula to integrate the Common Core State Standards. Prior to becoming an administrator, Mary taught a variety of high school English courses, instructed English as a Second Language courses at the college level, and was an adjunct professor in the Department of Family and Child Studies at Montclair State University.

Acknowledgments

I would like to thank my family, friends, and colleagues for their support in this endeavor.

M.D.

I would like to thank Peter Mavrikis for all his support for this project.

T.H.

All inquiries should be addressed to:
Barron's Educational Series, Inc.
250 Wireless Boulevard
Hauppauge, NY 11788
www.barronseduc.com

ISBN: 978-1-4380-0564-5

Library of Congress Control Number 2014949909

Printed in the United States of America

9 8 7 6 5 4 3 2 1

10% POST-CONSUMER WASTE
Paper contains a minimum of 10% post-consumer waste (PCW). Paper used in this book was derived from certified, sustainable forestlands.

Contents

Chapter 1
What Is PARCC?   **1**

- New Standards in American Education   1
- A New Test for the New Standards   1
- How PARCC Is Given   1
- When PARCC Is Given   4
- The Performance-Based Assessment (PBA)   5
- The End-of-Year Assessment (EOY)   5
- How Are Students Scored? (PLD)   5
- Chapter Review   6

Chapter 2
Reading   **7**

- Understanding the Setup   7
- Reading Selections   7
- Types of Questions   12
- Practice and Develop Strategies with a Short Reading   20
- Practice on Your Own   33

Chapter 3
The Narrative Writing Task   **49**

- Your Chance to Be Creative   49
- Tips for Evaluating a Prompt   49
- Speculating About Text   50
- Narrative Writing Task #1   52
- Narrative Writing Task #2   58
- Narrative Writing Task #3   63
- Chapter Review   66

Chapter 4
The Literary Analysis Task   **67**

- Comparing and Contrasting Two Texts   67
- Before You Read   67

- As You Read 68
- After You Read 74
- The Outline 76
- Writing the Essay 79
- Chapter Review 81

Chapter 5
The Research Simulation Task   83

- Write a Mini Research Paper 83
- Read the Directions 85
- Use the Questions on the Test to Gather Information ... 86
- Read the Essay Question Carefully 89
- Plan to Write the Essay 90
- Writing Your Thesis 93
- The Body Paragraphs 95
- The Introduction and Conclusion 96
- Working Through an RST 97
- Chapter Review 106

Chapter 6
Practice Test—Performance-Based Assessment   107

- Practice the PARCC Performance-Based Assessment 107
- Answers 149

Chapter 7
Practice Test—End-of-Year Assessment   161

- Practice the PARCC End-of-Year Assessment (Part One) .. 161
- Answers 175
- Practice the PARCC End-of-Year Assessment (Part Two) .. 178
- Answers 188

Appendix A: A Glossary of PARCC Terms   191

Appendix B: Condensed Scoring Rubric   195

Index   199

What Is PARCC?

New Standards in American Education

For years, news reports stated that American students were falling behind students in other countries. Since states, not the federal government, were in charge of education, each state created its own exam to check for student progress. Not all exams were the same difficulty, and it was hard to understand where American students were proficient.

In 2009, the National Governors Association had a group of educators convene to map out where students should be at each grade level. What they created is called the Common Core State Standards, or the Common Core for short. Forty-four of the fifty states and five U.S. territories adapted the Common Core standards.

A New Test for the New Standards

Once the Common Core was established, states took another look at what they were assessing and how they were assessing it. From that, and from a federal Race to the Top educational grant, PARCC was created in 2010.

PARCC means Partnership for Assessment of Readiness for College and Careers. It is designed to coincide with Common Core, and it is designed to replace all the individual state tests.

The first PARCC will be administered in the 2014 school year. Sixteen states plus the District of Columbia are in the PARCC consortium.

How PARCC Is Given

PARCC is not a paper and pencil test. Instead, it is taken on a computer with an Internet connection. It bills itself as the next generation of test.

The online testing system is called TestNav. Students will read passages and answer different types of questions on the computer. Let's take a look at some sample questions from the Performance-Based Assessment practice test. The full sample test is at *http://practice.parcc.testnav.com/*.

The first example is an Evidence-Based Constructed Response Question (EBCR). The EBCR has two parts. In Part A, the student answers a question from what he or she reads. This is a typical question for any standard reading test. However, the EBCR goes further. In Part B, the student must provide evidence to support the answer from Part A. (Also, note that the reading passage is in its own window and scrolls. This screen shot only shows the beginning of the passage.)

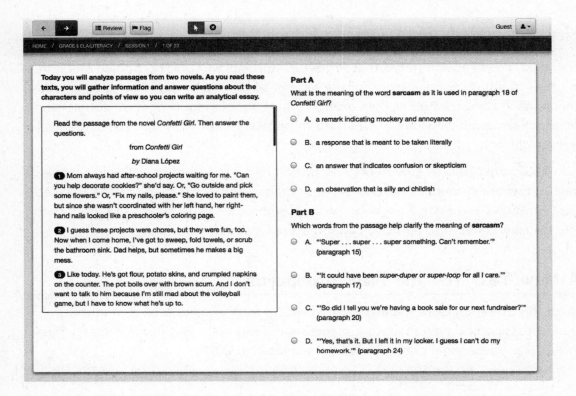

The next type of question is a Technology-Enhanced Constructed Response Question (TECR), where students are asked to click, select, highlight, and/or drag and drop. In the example on page 3, there are eight sentences. Students are asked to take five of the eight sentences and drag and drop them in order to make a summary of the passage. (Again, the story is in its own window and scrolls. Also, the five bubbles where the students drop the correct summary sentences are down the page and mostly out of view on this screen shot.)

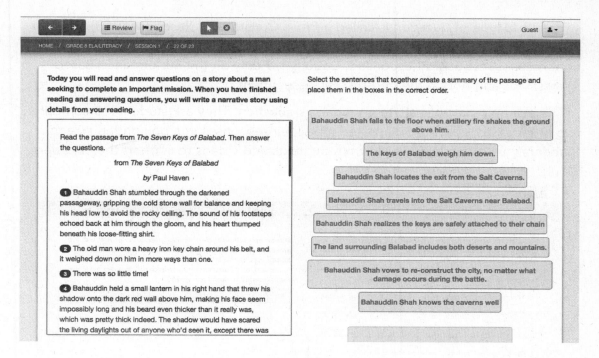

Below is another TECR. This question asks students to separate facts from opinions. Note that instead of a reading passage, students are asked to watch a video. The video is a big change from standardized tests of the past.

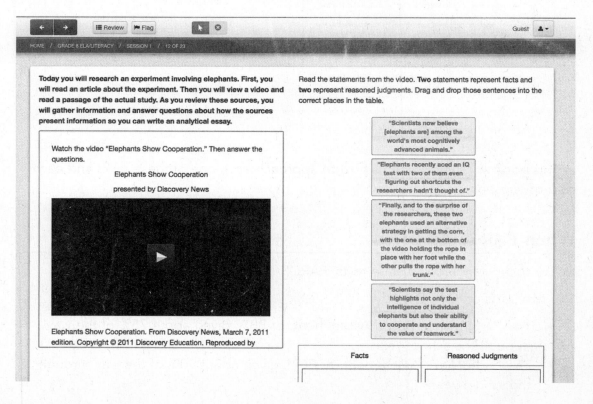

The third type of question is called a Prose Constructed Response (PCR). The three types of PCR questions are narrative, literary analysis, and research simulation. Prose Constructed Response questions are only on the Performance-Based Assessment and not on the End-of-Year Assessment.

The example below is a Literary Analysis question. They ask students to compare two or more texts and/or videos and type their responses in a box on the screen. Students must provide evidence from the texts and videos to support their answers.

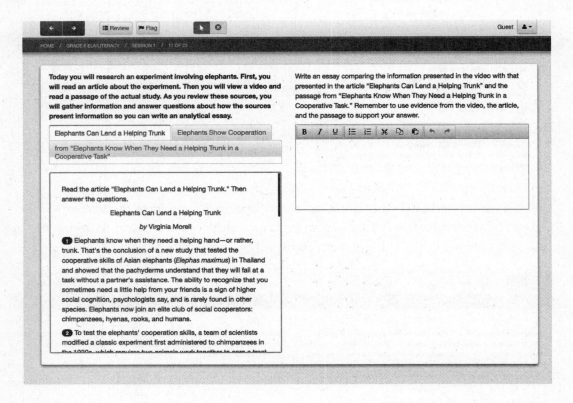

This book will show students how to approach each one of these tasks and each kind of question.

When PARCC Is Given

Unlike other standardized state tests, PARCC is given in two different sittings.

The two parts of PARCC are:

- The Performance-Based Assessment, or PBA, given about 75% of the way through the school year.
- The End-of-Year Assessment, or EOY, given about 90% of the way through the school year.

PARCC has two parts, math and English language arts (ELA for short). This book will focus on the English language arts portion of PARCC.

The Performance-Based Assessment (PBA)

The PBA, the first part of PARCC, is split into three parts, each of which will be covered in a separate chapter. The three parts are

- the Narrative Writing Task,
- the Literary Analysis Task, and
- the Research Simulation Task.

The PBA has both multiple-choice reading questions and extended writing sections.

The End-of-Year Assessment (EOY)

The EOY, the second part of PARCC, is given close to the end of the school year.

- Although there might be common elements from the narrative, literary, and research tasks, the main focus on the EOY will be reading comprehension.
- The EOY has two sections.

The PBA is the extended test that covers reading and extended writing, and the EOY is a little shorter, covering reading comprehension.

> **IMPORTANT NOTE:** Barron's has made every effort to ensure the content of this book is accurate as of press time, but the PARCC Assessments are constantly changing. Be sure to consult *www.parcconline.org* for all the latest testing information. Regardless of the changes that may be announced after press time, this book will still provide a strong framework for eighth-grade students preparing for the assessment.

How Are Students Scored? (PLD)

PARCC uses a combination of scoring to create a score called a Performance Level Descriptor, or PLD. Three categories are judged:

- text complexity,
- range of accuracy, and
- quality of evidence.

The three categories are combined to give an overall score, ranging from 1 to 5. The higher the score, the better.

- A 5 indicates a distinguished command of the language.
- A 4 indicates a strong command of the language.
- A 3 indicates a moderate command of the language.
- A 2 indicates a partial command of the language.
- A 1 indicates a minimal command of the language.

These PLD numbers and the scoring system are the same and consistent from year to year, so students will get used to the PARCC PLDs and what the numbers mean as they go through grade levels.

For a closer look into the scoring of the Reading and Writing sections of the PARCC exam, go to the following website:

http://www.parcconline.org/sites/parcc/files/Grade6-11-ELACondensed RubricFORANALYTICANDNARRATIVEWRITING.pdf

Note that each writing prompt (essay) is scored with this rubric, but the overall score (the reading and writing combined score of the entire test) is a score between 2 and 5. This overall test score is called a PLD.

CHAPTER REVIEW

> The PARCC was created to assess students' strengths and weaknesses in reading and writing.

> It emerged from a need to assess the Common Core, a new set of standards that aims to make clear what students should learn at each grade level.

> It is administered in two parts: the first part (the PBA) three-quarters of the way through the school year and the second part (the EOY) 90 percent of the way through the year.

> Instead of having separate reading and writing tasks, PARCC combines the two into tasks, where students have to read and write responses to what they have read.

> The tasks are scored using a chart that gives a scaled score from 1 to 5. This overall score is called a PLD.

Reading

CHAPTER 2

Understanding the Setup

There is a lot of reading on the Grade 8 PARCC exam. As we discussed earlier in Chapter 1, the PARCC exam has reading in the three sections of the Performance-Based Assessment (PBA) and in both sections of the End-of-Year Assessment (EOY). Depending on the section, you might be asked to compare texts, to determine what common themes are in texts, to analyze information across texts to form an argument, to determine what context clues led you to understanding the meaning of a vocabulary word, to explain what sentences support the topic sentence, or to demonstrate your understanding of what the text says by extending a story.

This might seem overwhelming, but you can master all of these. In this chapter, we will focus upon how to put your understanding to work for you in the multiple-choice questions, and in other chapters we will sharpen your writing skills.

Here is what we will do in this chapter:

1. Discuss the types of reading selections that you will see on the test.
2. Review some general tips for multiple-choice questions and new question types.
3. Practice and develop strategies with a short reading.
4. Practice on your own.

Reading Selections

The PARCC exam will have a variety of fiction and nonfiction works. You might see:

an excerpt from a novel or short story	a poem	an editorial or letter to an editor
an excerpt from an autobiography	an article	a speech made by a famous person
a review or first-hand account of an event	an interview	a description of a scientific process

The point is this: as long as you are an active reader who reads a variety of material regularly, you will continue to develop skills you need to succeed on this test. Much of the work that you have done in your English, history, and science classes has prepared you for the PARCC exam. This book is helping you to hone, or sharpen, those skills.

Let's take a look at a few examples of the reading selection types listed on page 7 and discuss what you might have looked for as you read.

An Excerpt from a Novel or a Short Story

Beth did have the fever, and was much sicker than anyone but Hannah and the doctor suspected. The girls knew nothing about illness, and Mr. Laurence was not allowed to see her, so Hannah had everything her own way, and busy Dr. Bangs did his best, but left a good deal to the excellent nurse. Meg stayed at home, lest she should infect the Kings, and kept house, feeling very anxious and a little guilty when she wrote letters in which no mention was made of Beth's illness. She could not think it right to deceive her mother, but she had been bidden to mind Hannah, and Hannah wouldn't hear of 'Mrs. March bein' told, and worried just for sech a trifle.'

Jo devoted herself to Beth day and night, not a hard task, for Beth was very patient, and bore her pain uncomplainingly as long as she could control herself. But there came a time when during the fever fits she began to talk in a hoarse, broken voice, to play on the coverlet as if on her beloved little piano, and try to sing with throat so swollen that there was no music left, a time when she did not know the familiar faces around her, but addressed them by wrong names, and called imploringly for her mother. Then Jo grew frightened, Meg begged to be allowed to write the truth, and even Hannah said she `would think of it, though there was no danger yet'. A letter from Washington added to their trouble, for Mr. March had had a relapse, and could not think of coming home for a long while.

This particular passage is an excerpt from *Little Women* by Louisa May Alcott. These first two paragraphs are the opening of Chapter 18.

You might not have ever read *Little Women*, but you might have picked out some features from this excerpt that you might have discussed about other books and stories in your English class. Did you notice how the author created:

- **Complex sentences:** "The girls knew nothing about illness, and Mr. Laurence was not allowed to see her, so Hannah had everything her own way, and busy Dr. Bangs did his best, but left a good deal to the excellent nurse."

- **A conflict:** "... feeling very anxious and a little guilty when she wrote letters in which no mention was made of Beth's illness. She could not think it right to deceive her mother, but she had been bidden to mind Hannah,...."

- **Context clues for challenging vocabulary words:** "...a time when she did not know the familiar faces around her, but addressed them by wrong names, and called imploringly for her mother."

- **Figurative language:** "to play on the coverlet as if on her beloved little piano,...."

- **Indirect characterization through dialogue:** "Mrs. March bein' told, and worried just for sech a trifle."

- **Direct characterization:** "Beth was very patient, and bore her pain uncomplainingly as long as she could control herself."

A Poem and Article

Sometimes the PARCC exam will pair poems, artwork, photographs, or a video with a nonfiction article. Here is an example of what that pairing might look like. The poem, "Theme in Yellow" by Carl Sandburg would be paired with a nonfiction article.

- "Theme in Yellow" is from *http://carl-sandburg.com/poem.htm*

Theme in Yellow

by Carl Sandburg

I spot the hills

With yellow balls in autumn.

I light the prairie cornfields

Orange and tawny gold clusters

And I am called pumpkins.

On the last of October

When dusk is fallen

Children join hands

And circle round me

Singing ghost songs

And love to the harvest moon;

I am a jack-o'-lantern

With terrible teeth

And the children know I am fooling.

Most likely, you have some level of familiarity with Halloween even though you might not have read the Sandburg poem before. Did you notice:

- **The setting of the poem?** (farmland in autumn until the end of October)

- **The changing point of view in the poem?** (first person point of view that begins as a pumpkin that dots the fields in yellow and orange and then becomes a jack-o-lantern that looks scary but children know it isn't)

- **How the poem tells the reader that Halloween is a time for children?** (Poem: "Children join hands/and circle round me/...children know I am fooling.")

As you can imagine, this poem might be paired with a video on the origins of Halloween, a picture of jack-o-lanterns, an artist's rendition of the poem, and/or a nonfiction article about Halloween. Here is a sample of what a nonfiction article about Halloween might look like:

Many people do not know the origins of Halloween. Although Halloween was not celebrated consistently in the colonies, autumn holidays were celebrated virtually everywhere in Colonial America.

There are some who speculate that the colonist and Native American traditions "meshed" to create an American holiday of Halloween. This theory is not well developed. One reason that this theory is not supported is that there are many different nations of Native Americans in the original colonies. These different nations each had different traditions and celebrations. It is not evident that any of these cultures celebrated a festival that involved children dressing up as spirits of the dead and soliciting candy from elders.

What is a more likely explanation is a combination of many different European celebrations brought to America. Many Americans think of the Pilgrims and the Puritan settlement of Boston when they think about the origins of America. The consideration of this New England settlement ignores the many other European cultures that settled in the New World: French, Dutch, Welsh, German, Irish, Swedish, and Spanish. It is well documented that these cultures celebrated the same Christian holidays but in different forms.

For a long time, Halloween was more about adults than children because of its religious associations. Many adults celebrated their deceased loved ones in Day-of-the-Dead celebrations on November 1st. However, some of these adult celebrations got rowdy; excessive drinking led to vandalism and other raucous behaviors. To curb this, many towns introduced trick-or-treating to get children involved.

Many communities liked the idea of getting children to participate in Halloween as a way of putting a halt on adult misbehavior. During the mid-century baby boom, children's participation in Halloween increased tremendously in communities across the country. Young and old alike celebrated Halloween with activities like apple bobbing, costume parties, haunted houses, and trick-or-treating.

As the baby boomers aged, they shared their childhood traditions with their own children; now these baby boomers are grandparents, and their grandchildren are celebrating the holiday. Not surprisingly, sales of costumes, make-up, and of course, candy, have soared in recent years. Currently, Halloween is the second most commercial holiday in the United States.

Again, there are many more types of reading selections that you may see, but by now you should have a pretty good idea of what the questions on the PARCC exam will ask you. Let's discuss those in a little more detail.

Types of Questions

Multiple-Choice Questions and New Question Types

By eighth grade, you are pretty familiar with how your teachers create tests. You have mastered

- the true and false question,

    1. T/F George Washington is still alive.

- the "place-the-events-in-chronological-order" question (also known as the sequence question),

    2. Please order the events by placing the number in which they occurred in the blank.

    _____ I took the milk carton out of the refrigerator.

    _____ I was thirsty.

    _____ I opened the refrigerator.

    _____ I drank a glass of milk.

- the matching question,

    3. Please match the vocabulary word to its meaning.

    A. agrarian   bitter hatred
    B. zeal   strong
    C. stalwart   enthusiasm
    D. acrimony   farm life

- the fill-in-the-blank question,

4. The _____ must be to provide the best education in the most effective manner to the children of New Jersey.

    ○ A. opponent
    ○ B. goal
    ○ C. challenge
    ○ D. conflict

- the multiple-choice question,

5. According to the poem, if you carve a pumpkin, it is called

    ○ A. an orange ball
    ○ B. a jack-o-lantern
    ○ C. a pumpkin pie
    ○ D. a tricky treat

- and the tricky multiple-choice question,

6. The author of "Theme in Yellow" makes all of the following points EXCEPT

    ○ A. Pumpkins look like yellow orbs.
    ○ B. Pumpkins make farmland look dark and dreary.
    ○ C. Children join hands around pumpkins and sing songs at Halloween.
    ○ D. Children know that jack-o-lanterns aren't really scary.

Answers

1. **F**

2. **{3, 1, 2, 4}**

3. **agrarian = farm life, zeal = enthusiasm, stalwart = strong, acrimony = bitter hatred;**

4. **B**

5. **B**

6. **B**

The good news for you is that the PARCC exam has many of these same question types; they might look a little different because they are on the computer, but we will show you what you might see and discuss how you should answer the questions. We pulled out many of the items your English teacher may have discussed with you if you read these pieces in class. Again, the PARCC will ask you about these items, too.

The first strategy for the PARCC is the easiest strategy to master:

> ## READ THE TEXT.

The makers of the PARCC exam won't give you a reading comprehension question on something you have not read. The answer will always be in the reading. It's up to you to find it.

One major change from your teachers' tests that you may notice is that the PARCC exam will have two-part questions. You might be asked to provide the context clues that led you to determine what the meaning was or where the support was in an essay. For example, in question 5, you were asked to complete a sentence about what pumpkins are called at Halloween. A follow-up question to that might look like this:

Which of the following supports your response for question 5?

- ○ **A.** The author personifies the pumpkin in line 12 when he says, "I am jack-o'-lantern."
- ○ **B.** The author explains that the children are joining hands and singing songs.
- ○ **C.** The author describes the harvest moon in line 11.
- ○ **D.** The author says that he lights up the fields in line 3.

Vocabulary Questions

You might be asked to determine the meaning of words or phrases from the text. When you read on a regular basis, you use context clues to determine what the word means.

You will probably know most of the words that the PARCC will ask you to define. The trick is that they may ask you *how* the word is used. This means that they are asking you how the author uses the word, regardless of what the word might actually mean. This is done frequently with figurative language. For example, an author might say that the character "thundered out of the room." If the PARCC asked you to define the word **thundered**, you would not respond that the character caused a storm. The text may describe other actions that the character might have taken; he may have grumbled loudly, walked heavily, and slammed the door on his way out of the room. The grumbling voice, booming steps, and slamming door would create an image of thunder.

You may also have to rely on the context to determine the connotation of a word. The connotation means that the vocabulary word might have more meaning than what you might find in the dictionary. For instance, if you looked up the word *surprise* in the dictionary, you would find, "an expected or astonishing event, fact, or thing." Examine how the word *surprise* is used in the following two sentences:

> Sentence One: My mother said that she had a surprise waiting for me when I got home.
>
> Sentence Two: The neighbor's dog left a surprise on our lawn.

Which surprise would you like?

Hopefully, you've used the contexts of those sentences to make your choice.

Main Idea and Summarizing Questions

Imagine that you have read a poem, watched a video, or read a nonfiction article about Halloween. You might receive a question that asks you to create a summary based upon what you have read or viewed. The exam will ask you to "drag and drop" statements into chronological order. It might look like:

From the list, create a summary by dragging the four most important statements and dropping them in chronological order in the table.

- For many years, only adults celebrated Halloween at community functions.
- Incidents of vandalism declined as trick-or-treating was introduced as a way to involve more families in the celebration.
- The baby boom contributed to the holiday becoming a child-centered than adult-centered holiday.
- A lot of businesses make money from sales of cards, candy, and costumes in October.
- Although Halloween was not celebrated consistently in the colonies, autumn holidays were celebrated virtually everywhere.
- Unfortunately, when the entire town celebrated the holiday, there was a lot of mischief and vandalism.

Event 1	
Event 2	
Event 3	
Event 4	

As you read back your answer to check your response, it should sound like a coherent paragraph:

Although Halloween was not celebrated consistently in the colonies, autumn holidays were celebrated virtually everywhere. For many years, only adults celebrated Halloween at community functions. Unfortunately, when the entire town celebrated the holiday, there was a lot of mischief and vandalism. Incidents of vandalism declined as trick-or-treating was introduced as a way to involve more families in the celebration.

You also may be asked to consider using the reading passages or video to create an argument and select evidence from the article to support your response. Often times, the PARCC will ask you to drag and drop more than one piece of evidence.

Part A

Below are three claims that could be made based on the article you read. Select the claim that is supported by the *most* relevant and sufficient evidence within the article. The claim you select will be highlighted in yellow.

Claim One	An "American" Halloween is a holiday that recognizes the traditions of many cultures.
Claim Two	Halloween sales have helped many small businesses survive.
Claim Three	Halloween parties have traditionally focused upon magic and witchcraft.

Part B

Select evidence paraphrased from the article that *best* supports the answer in Part A. Drag two sentences from the list and drop them into the Evidence Box.

At the turn of the century, Halloween parties for both children and adults became the most common way to celebrate the day.

As the beliefs and customs of different European ethnic groups mixed, a distinctly American version of Halloween began to emerge.

Parties focused on games, foods of the season, and festive costumes.

Today, Americans spend billions annually on Halloween, making it the country's second largest commercial holiday.

Young women believed that on Halloween they could divine the name or appearance of their future husband by doing tricks with yarn, apple parings, or mirrors.

EVIDENCE BOX

Answers: **"As the beliefs…"** and **"At the turn of the century…."**

Supporting Details

You might be asked to look at how an essay or a paragraph are structured, and then asked to explain your answer. We've reprinted paragraphs 4 and 5 from the Halloween article you read earlier.

> For a long time, Halloween was more about adults than children because of its religious associations. Many adults celebrated their deceased loved ones in Day-of-the-Dead celebrations on November 1st. However, some of these adult celebrations got rowdy; excessive drinking led to vandalism and other raucous behaviors. To curb this, many towns introduced trick-or-treating to get children involved.
>
> Many communities liked the idea of getting children to participate in Halloween as a way of putting a halt on adult misbehavior. During the mid-century baby boom, children's participation in Halloween increased tremendously in communities across the country. Young and old alike celebrated Halloween with activities like apple bobbing, costume parties, haunted houses, and trick-or-treating.

Part A

Which sentence demonstrates a cause and effect relationship?

○ A. Many adults celebrated their deceased loved ones in Day-of-the-Dead celebrations on November 1st.
○ B. However, some of these adult celebrations got rowdy; excessive drinking led to vandalism and other raucous behaviors.
○ C. Many communities liked the idea of getting children to participate in Halloween as a way of putting a halt on adult misbehavior.
○ D. Young and old alike celebrated Halloween with activities like apple bobbing, costume parties, haunted houses, and trick-or-treating.

Part B

Which of the following choices best supports your selection for Part A?

○ A. The author explains why the Day-of-the-Dead festival was so important to the European settlers.
○ B. The author categorizes a type of behavior, then states that one activity contributed to this behavior.
○ C. The author suggests having child-centered activities was appealing because children are cute.
○ D. The author suggests that children's activities were more interesting and less harmful than adults' activities.

Answers: Part A: **B** and Part B: **B**.

Here are some general strategies that will serve you well on this test:

1. **As you read the text selections, take notes.** You will have a notepad on your computer that will allow you to jot down your ideas as you read. Look for points that the authors make, figurative language, topic sentences, supporting statements, thesis statements, and make short summaries of longer paragraphs. In essence, you are creating a guide for yourself so that when you return to the text to answer the questions, you can get to those answers quickly.

   If you are not in the habit of doing this already, please start now. If you can't write in your textbook, have your notebook open next to it, write the page number down, and write your comments as you read.

   If you have an electronic reading device, practice highlighting information and commenting on it electronically.

2. **Return to the text to answer your questions.** There is a lot of information in the text, and, because you took notes, you know right where to find it.

3. **Build your vocabulary.** Part of this test is understanding and using academic vocabulary words. When you read a story, write down any words you don't know immediately and make them yours! Find ways to use them when you write, when you talk to your teachers, and when you speak to your parents (dazzle them!).

   Almost as important as knowing words on sight is knowing how to determine a word's meaning from context. If you can, underline the context clues or write them in your notebook. If you are using an electronic reader and are used to pressing a word to have the definition provided to you, that is fine, but take it a step further and highlight the context clues that led you to the definition.

Practice and Develop Strategies with a Short Reading

Let's do some practice with the new types of PARCC questions that you will see on the test. We'll get a fresh article for you to read. This article is from *National Geographic Magazine* and is online at http://ngm.nationalgeographic.com/2013/11/new-america-map/ballard-text.

New America

Robert Ballard embarks on a ten-year expedition to discover what lies beneath the waves of this country's latest frontier.

By Robert D. Ballard

November 2013

America has had two great ages of exploration. The one that every schoolchild learns about began in 1804, when Thomas Jefferson sent Meriwether Lewis and William Clark on their epic journey across North America. The other one is just beginning. During this new age of exploration we will go farther than Lewis and Clark and learn the secrets of territories beyond even Jefferson's wildest imagination. Yet it seems safe to say that most Americans don't know anything about it.

Few realize that the single largest addition to the American domain came on March 10, 1983, when President Ronald Reagan, with the stroke of a pen, expanded the country's sovereign rights 200 nautical miles from its shores "for the purpose of exploring, exploiting, conserving, and managing natural resources." By establishing an exclusive economic zone (EEZ), Reagan roughly doubled the area within United States boundaries, as Jefferson had with the Louisiana Purchase.

Other countries have increased their jurisdiction over natural resources through EEZs and are eager to add more. Under the 1982 UN Convention on the Law of the Sea, which the United States has not joined, countries can claim sovereign rights over a larger region if they can prove that the continental shelf—the submerged portion of a continent—extends beyond their EEZ and meets certain other conditions. The United States potentially has one of the largest continental shelves in the world.

A lot is at stake. Just like the land that Lewis and Clark explored, the ocean floor contains natural resources, many of them untapped. Vast oil and gas deposits lie under the waves. So do hydrothermal vents, where copper, lead, silver, zinc, and gold have been accumulating for hundreds of millions of years. By some estimates there are more than 100,000 seamounts containing minerals critical for national defense. That's not all that lies beneath. These watery zones encompass fisheries that nations rely on for sustenance, shipwrecks that may reveal lost chapters of history, and habitats that need to be preserved as marine sanctuaries.

Most of the U.S. EEZ hasn't been explored. In 1803, with the territory from the Louisiana Purchase newly in hand, Jefferson instructed expedition leader Lewis to "take observations on ... the soil & face of the country, its growth & vegetable productions ... the mineral productions of every kind ... volcanic appearances [and] climate as characterized by the thermometer."

Reagan did not follow Jefferson's example. To this day we have better maps of Venus, Mars, and the far side of the moon than we do of much of underwater America.

But now it's time for a new epic journey. Last June the United States' only dedicated ships of exploration launched a joint, concentrated effort to find out what lies within the country's EEZ. The National Oceanic and Atmospheric Administration's *Okeanos Explorer* mapped some of the New England Seamount chain near Rhode Island, among other places, while my vessel—the Ocean Exploration Trust's *Nautilus*—mapped portions of the Gulf of Mexico and the Caribbean. Both ships use multibeam sonars mounted on their hulls, which enable the creation of maps in three dimensions.

Lewis and Clark traveled for more than two years and had to wait until their return home to share their discoveries with an expectant nation. Although the ocean depths plumbed by these modern expeditions are more remote than the land Lewis and Clark charted, we are in constant communication with oceanographers and other experts on shore. The moment a discovery is made, scientists can step aboard either of the two ships virtually, take over operations, and share findings in real time with a plugged-in world. This is a voyage of discovery everyone can make.

Vocabulary Questions

Like many questions on the PARCC exam, the vocabulary questions will come in two parts, Part A and Part B. Part A will ask you what the vocabulary word means in context; Part B will ask what context clues led you to choose an answer in Part A.

It is possible to get one part right and the other part wrong. Again, when you read for your classes and you encounter a word with which you are not familiar, look for the context clues; highlight or underline them.

Think of these questions as fill-in-the-blank questions.

Strategy:

As you read the bolded word, think "_____." Fill in the blank with a word you know, and then match your word to the answer choices. Let's practice that here. We've blanked the word in context, **epic**, for the sake of this exercise.

Part A

Read the following excerpt from paragraph 1, reprinted here:

> The one that every schoolchild learns about began in 1804, when Thomas Jefferson sent Meriwether Lewis and William Clark on their _____ journey across North America. The other one is just beginning. During this new age of exploration we will go farther than Lewis and Clark and learn the secrets of territories beyond even Jefferson's wildest imagination.

The blank is looking for a word to describe Lewis and Clark's journey. You might have learned about it in history class, but in case you never heard of Lewis and Clark or their journey, take a look at some of the context clues surrounding the blank.

> …one that every school child learns about…new age of exploration…. beyond even Jefferson's wildest imagination.

It would stand to reason that if everyone learns about this journey, that the journey was exploratory, and it was beyond President Jefferson's imagination, that the journey had to be pretty big and important. So, we might think of a word for big and important, a word like *legendary*. Does it make sense when we insert it into the sentence? Let's try:

> The one that every schoolchild learns about began in 1804, when Thomas Jefferson sent Meriwether Lewis and William Clark on their **legendary** journey across North America. The other one is just beginning. During this new age of exploration we will go farther than Lewis and Clark and learn the secrets of territories beyond even Jefferson's wildest imagination.

Okay, it seems to make sense. Let's match our word to the answer choices.

A. inconsequential
B. monumental
C. mandatory
D. cooperative

The answer choice that is closest to our word, *legendary*, is **B.**, *monumental*. Answer choice A means that the journey was not important (without consequence), choice C means that they were forced, or mandated, to go on a journey, and choice D indicates that Lewis and Clark cooperated with someone (each other? Jefferson?).

If you don't know what the words mean, eliminate the words that you know are NOT the right choices and make a guess from there. You might have known the word *cooperative*, so you would not have chosen answer choice D. If you are not able to identify the vocabulary words in the answer choices, you might get the answer wrong for Part A, but, at least you were able to identify the context clues, which means that you can still get Part B right.

What happens if you couldn't come up with a word like *legendary* to fill in the blank? Don't panic. Fill in the blank with the words that you know. You might get answer choices that are phrases instead of one-word responses. Let's try the same strategy with our original response, "big and important."

The one that every schoolchild learns about began in 1804, when Thomas Jefferson sent Meriwether Lewis and William Clark on their **big and important** journey across North America. The other one is just beginning. During this new age of exploration we will go farther than Lewis and Clark and learn the secrets of territories beyond even Jefferson's wildest imagination. Yet it seems safe to say that most Americans don't know anything about it.

A. not important
B. grand and adventurous
C. made to go
D. helpful and promising

The response is the same, B, as it is closest to our answer, "big and important." As we move onto Part B, we should recognize the context clues that helped us get the right answer in A.

Part B

Which phrase from the article best helps you clarify the meaning of epic?

- ○ A. America has had two great ages of exploration.
- ○ B. The other one is just beginning.
- ○ C. During this new age of exploration we will go farther than Lewis and Clark and learn the secrets of territories beyond even Jefferson's wildest imagination.
- ○ D. Yet it seems safe to say that most Americans don't know anything about it.

Hopefully, you chose C. It has the most context clues that we identified earlier. The others do provide some context clues, but choice C has the most that directly relate to the meaning of the word in context.

Try one of these questions on your own. We'll reprint the paragraphs here. Ready?

Few realize that the single largest addition to the American domain came on March 10, 1983, when President Ronald Reagan, with the stroke of a pen, expanded the country's sovereign rights 200 nautical miles from its shores "for the purpose of exploring, exploiting, conserving, and managing natural resources." By establishing an exclusive economic zone (EEZ), Reagan roughly doubled the area within United States boundaries, as Jefferson had with the Louisiana Purchase.

Other countries have increased their **jurisdiction** over natural resources through EEZs and are eager to add more. Under the 1982 UN Convention on the Law of the Sea, which the United States has not joined, countries can claim sovereign rights over a larger region if they can prove that the continental shelf—the submerged portion of a continent—extends beyond their EEZ and meets certain other conditions. The United States potentially has one of the largest continental shelves in the world.

Part A

What is the meaning of the word **jurisdiction** as used in paragraph 3?

- ○ A. endorsement
- ○ B. rejection
- ○ C. dismay
- ○ D. command

Part B

Which phrase from the text best helps clarify the meaning of **jurisdiction**?

- ○ A. Few realize that the single largest addition to the American domain
- ○ B. as Jefferson had with the Louisiana Purchase.
- ○ C. Law of the Sea, ...countries can claim sovereign rights
- ○ D. one of the largest continental shelves in the world.

The answers are: Part A: **D** and Part B: **C**. In Part B, the words *sovereign* and Law should have helped you to determine that the passage was discussing some issue of determining what country rules a territory. Also, the word *sovereignty* is a synonym for *jurisdiction*. The word *domain* in answer choice A might have helped as well, but the whole phrase presented there does not necessarily refer to which country rules what, it refers to the size of the territory.

Main Idea and Summarizing Questions

These questions are a combination of a few types of questions: chronological order (or sequential order), identifying the main point, and finding supporting evidence. What these types of questions have in common is that they ask you to look carefully at the essay and, in some cases, determine how the essay is organized so that you can identify the main idea and the supporting evidence that the author has used.

The makers of the PARCC exam might provide you with some statements that summarize events found in the text. The idea is that these statements are what you might have said if you had to write a quick overview of what was in the selection.

To answer these questions, you have to have read the entire selection, paying special attention to the topic sentences and the organization of the essay. Authors frequently organize essays from the least important event to the most significant event, so if you just read the first part of an essay, you will miss out on something major.

This particular essay is a comparative essay, that is, it will compare one thing with another. In this case, what are being compared are two journeys: the one that Lewis and Clark made and the one that our author, scientist Robert D. Ballard, is currently making as he explores the ocean floor.

How did we know that Ballard was the scientist making this expedition? We followed rule number one, go back to the text:

New America

Robert Ballard embarks on a ten-year expedition to discover what lies beneath the waves of this country's latest frontier.

By Robert D. Ballard

November 2013

In your classes, you might analyze a comparison by using a Venn diagram. We can't do that on this test because we can't draw circles on the computer. What we will have to do instead is to approximate a Venn diagram by placing the points of comparison in the center and the evidence on either side. We can also use this strategy on the PARCC exam if you are asked to compare one passage to another. Our "charted" Venn diagram for this passage will look like this:

Lewis and Clark	Point of Comparison	Robert D. Ballard

Let's fill it in. It will help us to put in as many points of comparison that we can find equal evidence for.

Lewis and Clark	Point of Comparison	Robert D. Ballard
To explore territory over the land	**Purpose of exploration**	To explore territory under the sea
1804	**Time of exploration**	2013
1803: President Jefferson	**Time that president acquired territory**	1983: President Reagan
Untapped natural resources	**Why is the area important?**	Oil and gas deposits, minerals, fisheries, shipwrecks, habitats
Two years of traveling over the land, observation, thermometers	**Methods of discovery**	Ships traveling over the territory, scientists using technology to do virtual exploration
Lewis and Clark publish findings after a two-year journey	**Sharing discovery with the public**	Scientists provide pictures and commentary instantly online

Now that we know what is in the essay and can clearly see how it is organized, we are ready to answer any question that the PARCC exam can throw at us.

In the article, "New America," the author claims that the exploration of the newly-acquired territory in the ocean resembles Lewis and Clark's exploration of the Louisiana purchase. Which reasons support the author's claim that the exploration of the sea floor is similar to Lewis and Clark's exploration of the American continent? From the list, identify the three reasons that the author would agree with and drop them into the chart in their order of importance.

Reasons

The public could expect to move into the new areas as soon as they had been thoroughly explored.

Both President Reagan and President Jefferson thought that expansion was good for America.

We can learn new things about animals, minerals, and land by thoroughly exploring new territory on Earth.

Information about new territories might be slow in coming, but worth the wait.

The public has a right to know what the president has purchased.

Reason 1	
Reason 2	
Reason 3	

To answer this question, let's first identify what is asking of us before we go back to look at the chart that we made. It's asking us to determine which reasons support the author's claim. That means that we have to distinguish between what the author would agree with and what he would disagree with. Next, we have to put them in order of importance. That means we have to determine what the author would be behind strongly, then not as strongly, and finally still agree with but not as whole-heartedly.

Let's look at the reasons and use our chart to determine what the author would agree with first.

We notice that the first reason, "The public...," is not on our chart. In fact, that response makes little sense with what was provided in the essay. If you hadn't read the essay all of the way through, you might have selected that response because the discussion of the public was not made until the end of the essay.

Both presidents are mentioned in our chart ("Both President Reagan and Jefferson..."). We have who acquired the territory and when, but our chart doesn't have the why. We're going to take a quick look back in the text. Jefferson bought the Louisiana Purchase to expand the country, the purchase was made in 1803, and Jefferson sent Lewis and Clark on their journey in 1804. In contrast, Reagan did not buy the underwater territory when he expanded the border, he did it in 1983, but the area was not explored until 2013. The author makes the comment that Reagan did not follow Jefferson's example, that he spent the money on space exploration instead. That leads us to believe that maybe Reagan thought that expansion into the sea was not the priority that Jefferson believed his purchase was, but this did not mean that Reagan did not believe that it was important for America. Look back again. Paragraph 2 has a quote from Ronald Reagan, the zone was expanded for, "exploring, exploiting, conserving, and managing natural resources." Clearly, he believed that this acquisition was important for the country.

Both of the explorations do expand upon the third reason, "We can learn...." We don't know the order of the importance yet, but this is definitely one of the reasons that we want to keep. There is evidence in the text supporting this statement on both sides of the chart.

The fourth reason, "Information about new territories...," is mentioned. Is it worth the wait? Waiting for the information is in both of our columns. For Lewis and Clark, they didn't have to wait to explore, but they did have to wait to provide information to the public. For Ballard, the wait is for the actual exploration, but not to provide information to the public. This is another one that we want to keep.

The final reason, "The public has a right to know...," is not discussed in the essay. We're going to eliminate this one.

Now that we have our three reasons, we have to prioritize them into order of importance. What is the most important reason that the sea floor exploration is similar to Lewis and Clark's exploration? Which would the author agree with the most? Let's look at our choices:

- Both President Reagan and President Jefferson thought that expansion was good for America.
- We can learn new things about animals, minerals, and land by thoroughly exploring new territory on Earth.
- Information about new territories might be slow in coming, but worth the wait.

Looking at our reasoning above, we can definitely say that there is concrete evidence in the essay to support the second reason, "We can learn..." in both explorations. That will be our first response.

The second reason that supports the idea of learning is "Information about new territories…." It is acknowledged in the chart that it took time, in both cases, to get the information, but for different reasons. However, Lewis and Clark would agree with Ballard that the information gained was very valuable.

Finally, we will order "Both President Reagan…" last. We had a little more time finding the support from Reagan as Ballard provided a criticism of him.

Now that we have it, our chart will look like this:

Reason 1	We can learn new things about animals, minerals, and land by thoroughly exploring new territory on Earth.
Reason 2	Information about new territories might be slow in coming, but worth the wait.
Reason 3	Both President Reagan and President Jefferson thought that expansion was good for America.

We can use our chart to answer a "claim" question. Let's repeat our notes before we see the question.

Lewis and Clark	Point of Comparison	Robert D. Ballard
To explore territory over the land	Purpose of exploration	To explore territory under the sea
1804	Time of exploration	2013
1803: President Jefferson	Time that president acquired territory	1983: President Reagan
Untapped natural resources	Why is the area important?	Oil and gas deposits, minerals, fisheries, shipwrecks, habitats
Two years of traveling over the land, observation, thermometers	Methods of discovery	Ships traveling over the territory, scientists using technology to do virtual exploration
Lewis and Clark publish findings after a two-year journey	Sharing discovery with the public	Scientists provide pictures and commentary instantly online

Here's the question:

Part A

Below are three claims that could be made based on the article "New America."

Claim One	There are many reasons why Americans should be interested in exploration.
Claim Two	Jefferson did more to help the United States than Reagan did.
Claim Three	When the country gains new territory, it is important to explore it to learn the potential.

Select the claim that is supported by the most relevant and sufficient evidence within the article "New America." The claim that you select will be highlighted in yellow on the computer exam.

Part B

Select the evidence from the article that best supports the answer in Part A. Drag two sentences from the list and drop them into the Evidence Box.

> Yet is seems safe to say that most American's don't know anything about it.

> By establishing an exclusive economic zone (EEZ), Reagan roughly doubled the area within the United Sates boundaries, as Jefferson had with the Louisiana Purchase.

> These watery zones encompass fisheries that nations rely on for sustenance, ship-wrecks that may reveal lost chapters of history, and habitats that need to be pre-served as marine sanctuaries.

> The United States potentially has one of the largest continental shelves in the world.

> Just like the land that Lewis and Clark explored, the ocean floor contains natural resources, many of them untapped.

> To this day we have better maps of Venus, Mars, and the far side of the moon than we do of much of underwater America.

> Lewis and Clark traveled for more than two years and had to wait until their return home to share their discoveries with an expectant nation.

```
┌─────────────────────────────────────────────────────┐
│                    EVIDENCE BOX                      │
│                                                       │
│                                                       │
│                                                       │
│                                                       │
│                                                       │
│                                                       │
│                                                       │
│                                                       │
│                                                       │
└─────────────────────────────────────────────────────┘
```

We were asked to determine which claim had the most evidence behind it. A quick look at our chart reveals that most of the points of comparison are on the exploration. Our evidence best supports Claim Three.

We are going to double-check Claim One and Claim Two to ensure that we have chosen the right response. Claim One was, "There are many reasons why Americans should be interested in exploration." While this might be true, it is not supported by the evidence that we collected. The essay is more about what can be learned than whether or not Americans should be interested in exploration.

Claim Two was, "Jefferson did more to help the United States than Reagan did." This is an opinion that is not supported. There are many comparisons between Jefferson and Reagan in the essay, but the author only says that Reagan did not follow Jefferson's example.

Let's look at the evidence now. We need something that will accompany our claim, "When the country gains new territory, it is important to explore it to learn the potential." We need evidence to support learning.

The two evidence statements that are most related to learning are, "These watery zones encompass fisheries that nations rely on for sustenance, shipwrecks that may reveal lost chapters of history, and habitats that need to be preserved as marine sanctuaries," and "Just like the land that Lewis and Clark explored, the ocean floor contains natural resources, many of them untapped." Both of these statements correlate to why it is important to explore new land.

The other statements discuss Americans' awareness of the land, a comparison of Reagan's decision to Jefferson's purchase, the size of the land, maps of extraterrestrial lands, and the timing of Lewis and Clark sharing their discovery.

Supporting Details Questions

Many times, the PARCC exam will ask you how a quotation or phrase contributes to the meaning of the text; Part B might ask you to identify how another section of the text makes a similar contribution. Let's try one together:

Part A

In paragraph 2 of "New America," Ballard uses a quote from President Reagan that explains the purpose of expanding the country's borders into the sea, "exploring, exploiting, conserving, and managing natural resources." How does the quotation contribute to the meaning of the paragraph?

- ○ A. It provides an example of Reagan's ambition to make the country larger.
- ○ B. It demonstrates that Reagan wanted to test the relationships with America's neighbors.
- ○ C. It illustrates that Reagan thought that the expansion could benefit America.
- ○ D. It suggests that natural resources in the ocean could not be protected without Reagan's declaration.

   The correct answer is **C** because the quotation specifically discusses what Reagan's intentions were when he acquired the territory. Choice A is not right because the rest of the paragraph, or article for that matter, does not discuss what Reagan's ambitions were. Choice B is not correct; again, nothing is mentioned about America's neighbors. The UN is mentioned in the next paragraph, but the question asked us specifically about paragraph 2, not paragraph 3. Choice D is also not supported by the rest of the paragraph.

   Now that we have mastered that part, let's move to Part B.

Part B

In which other paragraph in the article does a first-hand source contribute to the reader's understanding of why it is important to investigate new territory?

- ○ A. paragraph 4
- ○ B. paragraph 5
- ○ C. paragraph 6
- ○ D. paragraph 7

The answer is **B**, paragraph 5, where we find a quotation from Jefferson. Paragraph 4 mentions what might be discovered in the territory. Paragraph 6 explains how and where the exploration is being conducted. Paragraph 7 contains an explanation of how the information was relayed to the public.

Practice on Your Own

During the nineteenth century, Britain's Poor Law Amendment Act was enacted to assist people who were in poverty. One of the institutions created during this time was the workhouse, a place where people in debt would perform excruciating work in exchange for meager accommodations.

The following passages discuss the treatment of children who lived in workhouses during the Victorian Era. The first passage is an excerpt from the article "Children in the Workhouse," published by Workhouses.org, a website maintained by Peter Higginbotham. This excerpt was obtained from the website http://www.workhouses.org.uk/education/. The second passage is an excerpt from *Oliver Twist*, a popular novel by Charles Dickens.

Passage One

Children featured relatively little in the 1834 Poor Law Amendment Act or in the rules and regulations for its implementation issued by the Poor Law Commissioners. The original scheme of classification of inmates categorized females under sixteen as "girls" and males under thirteen as "boys," with those aged under seven forming a separate class. It probably came as a surprise to the Commissioners that, by 1839, almost half of the workhouse population (42,767 out of 97,510) were children.

Children arrived in the workhouse for a number of reasons. If an able-bodied man was admitted to (or departed from) the workhouse, his whole family had to accompany him. Once inside, the family was split up, with each going to their own section. A child under seven could, if deemed **"expedient,"** be accommodated with its mother in the female section of the workhouse and even share her bed. She was supposed to have access to the child "at all reasonable times." Parents were allowed a daily "interview" with a child living in the same workhouse, or an "occasional" interview if the child was in a different workhouse or school. Much of this depended on the discretion of the Guardians—for example, a minimum length of the "interview" was not laid down.

In 1838, Assistant Commissioner Dr. James Phillips Kay noted that children who ended up in the workhouse included "orphans, or deserted children, or bastards, or children of idiots, or of cripples, or of felons." Such children were not in the minority: according to the 1909 Royal Commission, around half the children under the care of Boards of Guardians in the nineteenth century were without parents or close relatives. From as early as 1842, the Poor Law Commissioners advised Boards of Guardians that they might detain any orphan child under the age of sixteen in receipt of relief if they believed it might suffer injurious consequences by leaving the workhouse. The Poor Law Acts of 1889 and 1899 gave them similar powers in respect of children of parents who were either dead, or "unfit" to control them, for example because they were in prison, convicted of an offence against the child, mentally deficient, in detention under the 1898 Inebriates Act, or permanently disabled and in the workhouse.

Boards of Guardians frequently became the legal guardians of orphaned children until were old enough to enter employment, usually from the age of fourteen. The great majority of girls went into domestic service, while boys usually entered into whatever local employment was on offer or, in some cases, joined the army or navy. Unions had legal responsibility to keep a check on their welfare until they were sixteen, with the union relieving officer visiting them periodically during this period.

The physical conditions in which workhouse children ended up were often appalling. The Poor Law Commissioners' Fourth Annual Report in 1838 recorded a visit by a physician to the Whitechapel workhouse who witnessed:

> ...the pale and unhealthy appearance of a number of children in the workhouse, in a room called the Infant Nursery. These children appear to be from two to three years of age; they are 23 in number; they all sleep in one room, and they seldom or never go out of this room, either for air or for exercise.

In another part of the same workhouse, 104 girls slept four or more to a bed in a room 88 feet long, 16½ feet wide and 7 feet high. 89 of the 104 had, perhaps unsurprisingly, recently been attacked with fever.

The Poor Law Commissioners' orders relating to the operation of workhouses contained a single regulation relating to their education:

> The boys and girls who are inmates of the Workhouse shall, for three of the working hours, at least, every day, be instructed in reading, writing, arithmetic, and the principles of the Christian religion, and such other instruction shall be imparted to them as may fit them for service, and train them to habits of usefulness, industry, and virtue.

The education of pauper children came to be provided for in a number of different ways including workhouse schools, separate and district schools, cottage homes, training ships, and the use of local National Schools and Board Schools. Further information on each of these is provided on separate pages.

The use of corporal punishment was one area where strict rules did exist relating to the treatment of children. The regulations issued by the Poor Law Commissioners required that:

1. No child under twelve years of age shall be punished by confinement in a dark room or during the night.

2. No corporal punishment shall be inflicted on any male child, except by the Schoolmaster or Master.

3. No corporal punishment shall be inflicted on any female child.

4. No corporal punishment shall be inflicted on any male child, except with a rod or other instrument, such as may have been *approved* of by the Guardians or the Visiting Committee.

5. No corporal punishment shall be inflicted on any male child until two hours shall have elapsed from the commission of the offence for which such punishment is inflicted.

6. Whenever any male child is punished by corporal correction, the Master and Schoolmaster shall (if possible) be both present.

7. No male child shall be punished by flogging whose age may be reasonably supposed to exceed fourteen years.

As suggested by the last item in the above list, "flogging" could be administered to boys under fourteen.

Despite these strict regulations, numerous instances of cruelty and abuse of children came to light over the years. Many early instances were extensively reported by *The Times* which was firmly against the new poor law. For example, the edition of 25th August 1838 carried a long letter from a correspondent in Bath. It catalogued numerous complaints including a claim that he had "known a little boy of eight or nine years to be flogged most cruelly for three days successively, for his complaining to the guardians of his having been unjustly beaten." A study into 21 such *Times* reports found that 12 were largely false, 5 were largely correct, and 4 apparently went uninvestigated.

Question One

Part A

Which of the following claims is most strongly supported by evidence in the text?

Claim One	Half of the population of the workhouses was children under the age of fourteen.
Claim Two	Workhouses provided an education for children who would otherwise not have attended a school.
Claim Three	Boys and girls who lived in workhouses were employed when they were in their early teens.

Part B

Drag and drop two of the following pieces of evidence from the text that support the claim you selected. (For the sake of putting it on paper, record the letter.)

A. The original scheme of classification of inmates categorized females under sixteen as "girls" and males under thirteen as "boys," with those aged under seven forming a separate class.

B. Unions had legal responsibility to keep a check on their welfare until they were sixteen, with the union relieving officer visiting them periodically during this period.

C. Parents were allowed a daily "interview" with a child living in the same workhouse, or an "occasional" interview if the child was in a different workhouse or school.

D. The great majority of girls went into domestic service, while boys usually entered into whatever local employment was on offer or, in some cases, joined the army or navy.

E. The use of corporal punishment was one area where strict rules did exist relating to the treatment of children.

F. The education of pauper children came to be provided for in a number of different ways including workhouse schools, separate and district schools, cottage homes, training ships, and the use of local National Schools and Board Schools.

```
┌─────────────────────────────────────────────────────────┐
│                      EVIDENCE BOX                        │
│                                                          │
│                                                          │
│                                                          │
│                                                          │
│                                                          │
│                                                          │
│                                                          │
│                                                          │
└─────────────────────────────────────────────────────────┘
```

Question Two

Part A

In paragraph two, the word **expedient** most nearly means

- ○ A. fair
- ○ B. wise
- ○ C. convenient
- ○ D. worrisome

Part B

Which of the following from the passage best supports your response for the answer in Part A?

- ○ A. "Children arrived in the workhouse for a number of reasons."
- ○ B. "… be accommodated with its mother in the female section of the workhouse and even share her bed."
- ○ C. "….the family was split up, with each going to their own section."
- ○ D. "… a minimum length of the 'interview' was not laid down."

Question Three

Part A

In paragraph 5 of the excerpt, the author writes, "The physical conditions in which workhouse children ended up were often appalling." How does he support this claim?

- ○ A. He provides the rules and regulations that set limits on room sizes.
- ○ B. He explains a quotation from the law.
- ○ C. He contrasts a well-run workhouse with a poorly-run workhouse.
- ○ D. He includes a quotation from a physician's report.

Part B

What other details are present in this excerpt that suggest that the children were not treated well in a workhouse? Select all that apply.

- ☐ A. The boys and girls were placed into separate workhouses from each other.
- ☐ B. Husbands and wives were separated from each other, but they could still see their children.
- ☐ C. Many of the smaller children were not let out of a room to get exercise.
- ☐ D. Children who lived in workhouses received an education for only three hours a day.
- ☐ E. Many children became ill because of the conditions in the workhouse.
- ☐ F. There were allegations of child abuse in workhouses that were not investigated.

Question Four

Part A

Which sentence explains how paragraph 3 is important to the development of the ideas in "Children in the Workhouses"?

- ○ A. Paragraph 3 explains what the circumstances might be for a child to be in the workhouse without parents.
- ○ B. Paragraph 3 shows that children received better treatment in the workhouse than on the street.
- ○ C. Paragraph 3 quotes the laws in keeping children in workhouses beyond the age of 16.
- ○ D. Paragraph 3 provides an explanation of the legality of separating children from their parents.

Part B

Which quotation from paragraph 3 best supports the response to Part A?

- ○ A. "…they might detain any orphan child under the age of 16 in receipt of relief if they believed it might suffer injurious consequences by leaving the workhouse…."
- ○ B. "…respect of children of parents who were either dead, or 'unfit' to control them…."
- ○ C. "…according to the 1909 Royal Commission, around half the children under the care of Boards of Guardians in the nineteenth century were without parents or close relatives."
- ○ D. "…noted that children who ended up in the workhouse included 'orphans, or deserted children, or bastards, or children of idiots, or of cripples, or of felons'…."

Question Five

Part A

Paragraph 8 contains a list of the rules that governed corporal punishment. Which of the following sentences best explains why the author decided to place this subject toward the end of the excerpt?

○ A. The purpose of paragraph 8 is to introduce the allegations of abuse described in paragraph 9; paragraph 8 does this by explaining what the rules were.

○ B. Paragraphs 5, 6, and 7 describe the benefits of children living in the workhouse; therefore, paragraph 8 should begin with the detriments to children.

○ C. Corporal punishment has been a part of education for many years, so it is a natural progression of ideas to move from education to punishment.

○ D. In paragraph 7 the author conveys a sense of hope; the author contrasts that in paragraph 8 where he explains what really happened to children in a workhouse.

Part B

The article lacks transitions in many places, among them, between paragraphs 7 and 8. Which of the following transitions would best work between these two paragraphs, reprinted here?

> The education of pauper children came to be provided for in a number of different ways including workhouse schools, separate and district schools, cottage homes, training ships, and the use of local National Schools and Board Schools. Further information on each of these is provided on separate pages.
>
> The use of corporal punishment was one area where strict rules did exist relating to the treatment of children. The regulations issued by the Poor Law Commissioners required that:...

○ A. Children who worked hard seldom needed to be punished. Unfortunately, some children did face consequences for misbehavior.

○ B. Children who lived in the workhouse had a variety of educational opportunities, but only a few chances of being punished.

○ C. When children are in school, sometimes they act out and receive consequences.

○ D. The government knew that children would misbehave, so the consequences for hurting a child were dire.

Passage Two

Chapter II: Treats of Oliver Twist's growth, education, and board.

For the next eight or ten months, Oliver was the victim of a systematic course of treachery and deception. He was brought up by hand. The hungry and destitute situation of the infant orphan was duly reported by the workhouse authorities to the parish authorities. The parish authorities inquired with dignity of the workhouse authorities, whether there was no female then domiciled in "the house" who was in a situation to impart to Oliver Twist, the consolation and nourishment of which he stood in need. The workhouse authorities replied with humility, that there was not. Upon this the parish authorities magnanimously and humanely resolved, that Oliver should be "farmed," or, in other words, that he should be dispatched to a branch-workhouse some three miles off, where twenty or thirty other juvenile offenders against the poor-laws, rolled about the floor all day, without the inconvenience of too much food or too much clothing, under the parental superintendence of an elderly female, who received the culprits at and for the consideration of sevenpence-halfpenny per small head per week. Sevenpence-halfpenny's worth per week is a good round diet for a child; a great deal may be got for sevenpence-halfpenny, quite enough to overload its stomach, and make it uncomfortable. The elderly female was a woman of wisdom and experience; she knew what was good for children; and she had a very accurate perception of what was good for herself. So, she appropriated the greater part of the weekly stipend to her own use, and consigned the rising parochial generation to even a shorter allowance than was originally provided for them. Thereby finding in the lowest depth a deeper still; and proving herself a very great experimental philosopher. Everybody knows the story of another experimental philosopher who had a great theory about a horse being able to live without eating, and who demonstrated it so well, that he got his own horse down to a straw a day, and would unquestionably have rendered him a very spirited and rapacious animal on nothing at all, if he had not died, four-and-twenty hours before he was to have had his first comfortable bait of air. Unfortunately for the experimental philosophy of the female to whose protecting care Oliver Twist was delivered over, a similar result usually attended the operation of the system; for at the very moment when a child had contrived to exist upon the smallest possible portion of the weakest possible food, it did perversely happen in eight and a half cases out of ten, either that it sickened from want and cold, or fell into the fire from neglect, or got half-smothered by accident; in any one of which cases, the miserable little being was usually summoned into another world, and there gathered to the fathers it had never known in this.

Occasionally, when there was some more than usually interesting inquest upon a parish child who had been overlooked in turning up a bedstead, or inadvertently scalded to death when there happened to be a washing—though the latter accident was very scarce, anything approaching to a washing being of rare occurrence in the farm—the jury would take it into their heads to ask troublesome questions, or the parishioners would rebelliously affix their signatures to a remonstrance. But these impertinences were speedily checked by the evidence of the surgeon, and the testimony of the beadle; the former of whom had always opened the body and found nothing inside (which was very probable indeed), and the latter of whom invariably swore whatever the parish wanted; which was very self-devotional. Besides, the board made periodical pilgrimages to the farm, and always sent the beadle the day before, to say they were going. The children were neat and clean to behold, when they went; and what more would the people have!

It cannot be expected that this system of farming would produce any very extraordinary or luxuriant crop. Oliver Twist's ninth birthday found him a pale thin child, somewhat diminutive in stature, and decidedly small in circumference. But nature or inheritance had implanted a good sturdy spirit in Oliver's breast. It had had plenty of room to expand, thanks to the spare diet of the establishment; and perhaps to this circumstance may be attributed his having any ninth birthday at all. Be this as it may, however, it was his ninth birth-day; and he was keeping it in the coal-cellar with a select party of two other young gentlemen, who, after participating with him in a sound thrashing, had been locked up for atrociously presuming to be hungry, when Mrs. Mann, the good lady of the house, was unexpectedly startled by the apparition of Mr. Bumble, the beadle, striving to undo the wicket of the garden-gate.

"Goodness gracious! Is that you, Mr. Bumble, sir?" said Mrs. Mann, thrusting her head out of the window in well-affected ecstasies of joy. "(Susan, take Oliver and them two brats up stairs, and wash 'em directly.) My heart alive! Mr. Bumble, how glad I am to see you, sure-ly!"

Now, Mr. Bumble was a fat man, and a choleric; so, instead of responding to this open-hearted salutation in a kindred spirit, he gave the little wicket a tremendous shake, and then bestowed upon it a kick which could have emanated from no leg but a beadle's.

"Lor, only think," said Mrs. Mann, running out, —for the three boys had been removed by this time,——"only think of that! That I should have forgotten that the gate was bolted on the inside, on account of them dear children! Walk in, sir; walk in, pray, Mr. Bumble, do, sir."

Although this invitation was accompanied with a curtsey that might have softened the heart of a churchwarden, it by no means mollified the beadle.

"Do you think this respectful or proper conduct, Mrs. Mann," inquired Mr. Bumble, grasping his cane, "to keep the parish officers a waiting at your garden-gate, when they come here upon porochial business connected with the porochial orphans? Are you aweer, Mrs. Mann, that you are, as I may say, a porochial delegate, and a stipendiary?"

"I'm sure, Mr. Bumble, that I was only a telling one or two of the dear children as is so fond of you, that it was you a coming," replied Mrs. Mann with great humility.

Mr. Bumble had a great idea of his oratorical powers and his importance. He had displayed the one, and vindicated the other. He relaxed.

"Well, well, Mrs. Mann," he replied in a calmer tone; "it may be as you say; it may be. Lead the way in, Mrs. Mann, for I come on business, and have something to say."

Mrs. Mann ushered the beadle into a small parlour with a brick floor; placed a seat for him; and officiously deposited his cocked hat and cane on the table before him. Mr. Bumble wiped from his forehead the perspiration which his walk had engendered, glanced complacently at the cocked hat, and smiled. Yes, he smiled. Beadles are but men; and Mr. Bumble smiled.

"Now don't you be offended at what I'm a going to say," observed Mrs. Mann, with captivating sweetness. "You've had a long walk, you know, or I wouldn't mention it. Now, will you take a little drop of somethink, Mr. Bumble?"

"Not a drop. Not a drop," said Mr. Bumble, waving his right hand in a dignified, but placid manner.

"I think you will," said Mrs. Mann, who had noticed the tone of the refusal, and the gesture that had accompanied it. "Just a leetle drop, with a little cold water, and a lump of sugar."

Mr. Bumble coughed.

"Now, just a leetle drop," said Mrs. Mann persuasively.

"What is it?" inquired the beadle.

"Why, it's what I'm obliged to keep a little of in the house to put into the blessed infants' Daffy, when they ain't well, Mr. Bumble," replied Mrs. Mann as she opened a corner cupboard, and took down a bottle and glass. "It's gin. I'll not deceive you, Mr. B. It's gin."

"Do you give the children Daffy, Mrs. Mann?" inquired Bumble, following with his eyes the interesting process of mixing.

"Ah, bless 'em, that I do, dear as it is," replied the nurse. "I couldn't see 'em suffer before my very eyes, you know, sir."

"No;" said Mr. Bumble approvingly; "no, you could not. You are a humane woman, Mrs. Mann." (Here she set down the glass.) "I shall take a early opportunity of mentioning it to the board, Mrs. Mann." (He drew it towards him.) "You feel as a mother, Mrs. Mann." (He stirred the gin-and-water.) "I–I drink your health with cheerfulness, Mrs. Mann;" and he swallowed half of it.

"And now about business," said the beadle, taking out a leathern pocket-book. "The child that was half-baptized, Oliver Twist, is nine year old today."

"Bless him!" interposed Mrs. Mann, inflaming her left eye with the corner of her apron.

"And notwithstanding a offered reward of ten pound, which was afterwards increased to twenty pound. Notwithstanding the most superlative, and, I may say, supernat'ral exertions on the part of this parish," said Bumble, "we have never been able to discover who is his father, or what was his mother's settlement, name, or condition."

Mrs. Mann raised her hands in astonishment; but added, after a moment's reflection, "How comes he to have any name at all, then?"

The beadle drew himself up with great pride, and said, "I inwented it."

"You, Mr. Bumble!"

"I, Mrs. Mann. We name our fondlings in alphabetical order. The last was a S, –Swubble, I named him. This was a T, –Twist, I named him. The next one as comes will be Unwin, and the next Vilkins. I have got names ready made to the end of the alphabet, and all the way through it again, when we come to Z."

"Why, you're quite a literary character, sir!" said Mrs. Mann.

"Well, well," said the beadle, evidently gratified with the compliment; "perhaps I may be. Perhaps I may be, Mrs. Mann." He finished the gin-and-water, and added, "Oliver being now too old to remain here, the board have determined to have him back into the house. I have come out myself to take him there. So let me see him at once."

Question Six

Part A

Which of the following statements from Passage One are portrayed in Passage Two? Select all that apply.

- ☐ A. "The original scheme of classification of inmates categorized females under sixteen as 'girls' and males under thirteen as 'boys', with those aged under seven forming a separate class."
- ☐ B. "A child under seven could, if deemed 'expedient', be accommodated with its mother in the female section of the workhouse and even share her bed."
- ☐ C. "Boards of Guardians frequently became the legal guardians of orphaned children until were old enough to enter employment, usually from the age of fourteen."
- ☐ D. "These children appear to be from two to three years of age; they are 23 in number; they all sleep in one room, and they seldom or never go out of this room, either for air or for exercise."
- ☐ E. "No child under twelve years of age shall be punished by confinement in a dark room or during the night."
- ☐ F. "As suggested by the last item in the above list, 'flogging' could be administered to boys under fourteen."
- ☐ G. "had 'known a little boy of eight or nine years to be flogged most cruelly for three days successively, for his complaining to the guardians of his having been unjustly beaten.'"

Question Seven

Part A

In the first and second paragraphs, the author makes the analogy of

- ○ A. comparing the workhouse to a slaughterhouse.
- ○ B. comparing the workhouse to a farm.
- ○ C. comparing Mrs. Mann to a horse.
- ○ D. comparing Mr. Bumble to a philosopher.

Part B

Which of the following support the response to Part A?

- ○ A. Dickens relates a story of a horse that eats just one straw a day, which is similar to the way that Mrs. Mann is paid for her work.
- ○ B. Mr. Bumble has a glass of gin and water upon Mrs. Mann's insistence.
- ○ C. The children who enter the workhouse never come out of it.
- ○ D. In paragraph 3, Dickens makes a remark about the "crop" of children.

Question Eight

The following quotation from the chapter occurs when Mrs. Mann greets
Mr. Bumble:

> "Goodness gracious! Is that you, Mr. Bumble, sir?" said Mrs. Mann, thrust-
> ing her head out of the window in well-affected ecstasies of joy. "(Susan, take
> Oliver and them two brats up stairs, and wash 'em directly.) My heart alive!
> Mr. Bumble, how glad I am to see you, sure-ly!"

Why has the author included parentheses in the above excerpt?

- ○ A. Dickens is contrasting how she speaks to Mr. Bumble with her actions inside the house.
- ○ B. Dickens is showing what Mrs. Mann is saying to her helper and then speaking to Mr. Bumble.
- ○ C. Dickens is providing an example of what Mrs. Mann's usual behavior is like.
- ○ D. Dickens is establishing a parallel between what Mrs. Mann says to the chil-dren and what she says to the authorities.

Question Nine

Part A

According to the text, what is the purpose for Mr. Bumble's visit?

- A. He fancies Mrs. Mann and wants to have a drink with her.
- B. He has been told to explain to her how he chooses names for the children in the parish.
- C. He has come to get Oliver because the child has been deemed "too old" to be in the nursery.
- D. He has come to do an inquiry into her spending habits.

Part B

The answer for Part A is supported with which of the following statements?

- A. Mrs. Mann pours Mr. Bumble a drink of gin as she explains how she uses the drink for the children.
- B. Mr. Bumble explains that he has a name at the ready for each orphaned child in alphabetical order.
- C. Mr. Bumble says that the child is nine and should be in the workhouse.
- D. Dickens explains that Mrs. Mann keeps most of the money she receives for her own use and spends little on the children.

Question Ten

Part A

These three claims could be made about the themes in *Oliver Twist*. Choose the one that is most supported by the evidence in the excerpt from Chapter II.

Claim One	Dickens believed that the workhouses could use some improvement, but the people who cared for the children were doing the best that they could with the limited resources available to them.
Claim Two	The conditions in the workhouse and its nursery were so deplorable that it was surprising that many children survived the conditions there.
Claim Three	Children who were in poverty received better nourishment, housing, education, and discipline in a workhouse than they would if they had been living on the streets.

Part B

Drag and drop three of the following pieces of evidence from the text that support the claim you selected. (For the sake of putting it on paper, record the letter.)

A. The hungry and destitute situation of the infant orphan was duly reported by the workhouse authorities to the parish authorities.

B. ...where twenty or thirty other juvenile offenders against the poor-laws, rolled about the floor all day, without the inconvenience of too much food or too much clothing, under the parental superintendence of an elderly female,

C. ...for at the very moment when a child had contrived to exist upon the smallest possible portion of the weakest possible food, it did perversely happen in eight and a half cases out of ten, either that it sickened from want and cold, or fell into the fire from neglect, or got half-smothered by accident; in any one of which cases, the miserable little being was usually summoned into another world, and there gathered to the fathers it had never known in this.

D. ... it was his ninth birth-day; and he was keeping it in the coal-cellar with a select party of two other young gentlemen, who, after participating with him in a sound thrashing, had been locked up for atrociously presuming to be hungry,....

E. Mr. Bumble was a fat man, and a choleric; so, instead of responding to this open-hearted salutation in a kindred spirit, he gave the little wicket a tremendous shake, and then bestowed upon it a kick which could have emanated from no leg but a beadle's.

F. The children were neat and clean to behold, when they went; and what more would the people have!

G. "No;" said Mr. Bumble approvingly; "no, you could not. You are a humane woman, Mrs. Mann." (Here she set down the glass.) "I shall take a early opportunity of mentioning it to the board, Mrs. Mann." (He drew it towards him.) "You feel as a mother, Mrs. Mann." (He stirred the gin-and-water.) "I– I drink your health with cheerfulness, Mrs. Mann;" and he swallowed half of it.

H. "Oliver being now too old to remain here, the board have determined to have him back into the house. I have come out myself to take him there. So let me see him at once."

EVIDENCE BOX

Answers

Question	Part A	Part B
1	Claim 3	B, D
2	C	B
3	D	C, E, F
4	A	D
5	A	A
6	A, D	
7	B	D
8	B	
9	D	C
10	Claim 2	B, C, D

The Narrative Writing Task

CHAPTER 3

Your Chance To Be Creative

For some students, this section of the test will be a breeze. For others, it will seem like torture. The reason is that the narrative writing task requires you to think creatively. Based on the details of the prompt, you must imagine what might be happening. In any case, you need to use the details in the given story to back up what you write.

Students will be given 50 minutes to complete the narrative writing task. On the earlier versions of the state exams, students were either given a picture or a simple prompt and asked to create a story from it. With PARCC, students will have to read a story or a piece of a story and then create a new narrative that uses elements of that story in an original way. Instead of only being asked to write a story, students instead will be asked to do one of the following:

- Create a story using the characters, mood, and setting of the story given;
- Prepare an organized description of a scientific process; or
- Prepare a description of an historical account.

In short, students in the past were given a basic situation and were asked to then write a story based on it. Now, students will have to read a passage and then integrate it into one of three possible writing tasks. Any way it is asked, students still must prewrite in order to organize their thoughts about what they plan to write. Students who do not plan will not do as well as they could!

Tips for Evaluating a Prompt

On this exam, you will be asked to complete a writing task on a very specific prompt in 50 minutes. This task will either be *speculative* or *explanatory*. Either way, you will have to take what you have read and create something new from it. The prompt will be written in such a way that you are given a *specific task* to envision and imagine. The task will include what you have to use from the passage and how you are to use it (what the form of the writing should be). It is your chance to be creative and be a storyteller.

To do that, think about what you are given in the prompt, and think if the elements make a good story:

- Establishing the problem or what will drive the story,
- Showing rising action as the story builds,
- Bringing the story to a climax, and
- Concluding the story.

Without these elements, you will not have a good story, and you will not score well on the prompt.

Speculating About Text

To *speculate* means to form a hypothesis or an educated guess. You will speculate about the story based on what you have read. In social studies class, you use the Five W's when you tell about a current event. When you speculate about a text, you must make sure that you cover those Five W's:

- Who?
- What?
- When?
- Where?
- Why?

Each of the sample prompts in this chapter is accompanied by a suggested planning strategy for prewriting. Although you are not officially graded on prewriting, the test makers provide you with planning space throughout the test. They do this because they expect that a good writer will take the time to plan and organize. You cannot score your best without planning first! Choose the strategy with which you are most comfortable to prewrite. Keep in mind the scoring rubric, located in the appendix of this book. The easiest way to think of scoring rubric is as follows:

- 1 = D
- 2 = C
- 3 = B
- 4 = A

When you think of the scoring this way, it is much easier to understand why essays receive certain scores. You have written many things over your years in school, and now you are being asked to show your skills.

Have a Strategy

Because you are given only 50 minutes to write this piece, you must have a plan of action going into the test. You must practice beforehand to see which strategy is best for you. Pay close attention to the samples following each of the practice prompts. The scoring rubric is designed to reward you for what you do well and to give you every opportunity to succeed on the task. As such, you can write either a creative story or an expository PCR as long as your central focus answers the questions who? what? when? where? why? and how? about the prompt you are given. The test rewards students who *show that they understand what they have read and use it in their PCR*. Also, when you try something different and do not write the same type of story many other students write, you are taking **compositional risk**. If you have heard the term "think outside the box," you understand what compositional risk is. Try to approach your writing in a different way, or try to tell your story with a twist that the reader will not see coming. When you do this, it makes the writing more enjoyable and, therefore, better.

Show, Don't Tell

One other way to make your writing better is to **show** what is happening, not *tell* it. Consider the following examples.

Example One

Little Red Riding Hood did not recognize her grandmother. She asked her about her physical features until the wolf, disguised as her grandmother, announced that he was going to eat her.

Example Two

Little Red Riding Hood approached her grandmother. "Grandma, what big eyes you have!" she exclaimed.

"The better to see you with," the Wolf, disguised as her grandmother, replied.

"And what a big nose you have!" Red Riding Hood said.

"The better to smell you with," said the Wolf.

"And what big teeth you have!" Red Riding Hood exclaimed.

"The better to eat you with!" cried the Wolf as he leaped out of the bed.

Narrative Writing Task #1—Complete a Story

Directions: Today you will read from chapter one of the novel, Treasure Island, by Robert Lewis Stevenson. As you read, pay close attention to characterization, details, and conflict as you prepare to write a narrative story.

Squire Trelawney, Dr. Livesey, and the rest of these gentlemen having asked me to write down the whole particulars about Treasure Island, from the beginning to the end, keeping nothing back but the bearings of the island, and that only because there is still treasure not yet lifted, I take up my pen in the year of grace 17—and go back to the time when my father kept the Admiral Benbow inn and the brown old seaman with the sabre cut first took up his lodging under our roof.

I remember him as if it were yesterday, as he came plodding to the inn door, his sea-chest following behind him in a hand-barrow—a tall, strong, heavy, nut-brown man, his tarry pigtail falling over the shoulder of his soiled blue coat, his hands ragged and scarred, with black, broken nails, and the sabre cut across one cheek, a dirty, livid white. I remember him looking round the cover and whistling to himself as he did so, and then breaking out in that old sea-song that he sang so often afterwards:

"Fifteen men on the dead man's chest—

Yo-ho-ho, and a bottle of rum!"

in the high, old tottering voice that seemed to have been tuned and broken at the capstan bars. Then he rapped on the door with a bit of stick like a handspike that he carried, and when my father appeared, called roughly for a glass of rum. This, when it was brought to him, he drank slowly, like a connoisseur, lingering on the taste and still looking about him at the cliffs and up at our signboard.

"This is a handy cove," says he at length; "and a pleasant sittyated grog-shop. Much company, mate?"

My father told him no, very little company, the more was the pity.

"Well, then," said he, "this is the berth for me. Here you, matey," he cried to the man who trundled the barrow; "bring up alongside and help up my chest. I'll stay here a bit," he continued. "I'm a plain man; rum and bacon and eggs is what I want, and that head up there for to watch ships off. What you mought call me? You mought call me captain. Oh, I see what you're at—there"; and he threw down three or four gold pieces on the threshold. "You can tell me when I've worked through that," says he, looking as fierce as a commander.

And indeed bad as his clothes were and coarsely as he spoke, he had none of the appearance of a man who sailed before the mast, but seemed like a mate or skipper accustomed to be obeyed or to strike. The man who came with the barrow told us the mail had set him down the morning before at the Royal George, that he had inquired what inns there were along the coast, and hearing ours well spoken of, I suppose, and described as lonely, had chosen it from the others for his place of residence. And that was all we could learn of our guest.

He was a very silent man by custom. All day he hung round the cove or upon the cliffs with a brass telescope; all evening he sat in a corner of the parlour next the fire and drank rum and water very strong. Mostly he would not speak when spoken to, only look up sudden and fierce and blow through his nose like a fog-horn; and we and the people who came about our house soon learned to let him be. Every day when he came back from his stroll he would ask if any seafaring men had gone by along the road. At first we thought it was the want of company of his own kind that made him ask this question, but at last we began to see he was desirous to avoid them. When a seaman did put up at the Admiral Benbow (as now and then some did, making by the coast road for Bristol) he would look in at him through the curtained door before he entered the parlour; and he was always sure to be as silent as a mouse when any such was present. For me, at least, there was no secret about the matter, for I was, in a way, a sharer in his alarms. He had taken me aside one day and promised me a silver four-penny on the first of every month if I would only keep my "weather-eye open for a seafaring man with one leg" and let him know the moment he appeared. Often enough when the first of the month came round and I applied to him for my wage, he would only blow through his nose at me and stare me down, but before the week was out he was sure to think better of it, bring me my four-penny piece, and repeat his orders to look out for "the seafaring man with one leg."

How that personage haunted my dreams, I need scarcely tell you. On stormy nights, when the wind shook the four corners of the house and the surf roared along the cove and up the cliffs, I would see him in a thousand forms, and with a thousand diabolical expressions. Now the leg would be cut off at the knee, now at the hip; now he was a monstrous kind of a creature who had never had but the one leg, and that in the middle of his body. To see him leap and run and pursue me over hedge and ditch was the worst of nightmares. And altogether I paid pretty dear for my monthly four-penny piece, in the shape of these abominable fancies.

From chapter one, "The Old Sea-Dog at the Admiral Benbow," of *Treasure Island* by Robert Lewis Stevenson.

Time: 50 minutes

Directions: In this passage, the author develops a situation with a pirate coming to live with a young man and his family. Think about the tension that the pirate has created for the young man. Write an original story to continue where the passage ended. In your story, be sure to use what you have learned about the pirate and the young man as you tell what happens next.

Method #1: Creating an Outline

If you tend to be a logical or mathematical learner, the outline is best suited for you. It provides an organized and simple method for you to gather your thoughts. Be careful, though! Some people do not outline properly, or they don't understand the importance of sequencing. Do not confuse outlining with listing. One of the best forms of outlining to use when writing a story is the one that is often used to dissect a story that is being read. It follows this format:

Story Outline

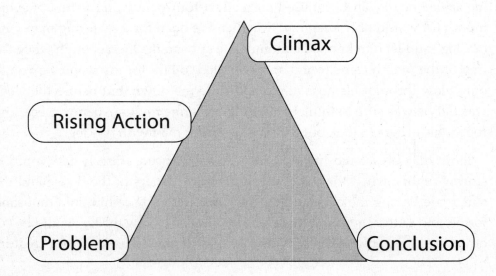

Now practice writing a sample outline for the prompt on page 54:

Sample Story Ending Outline

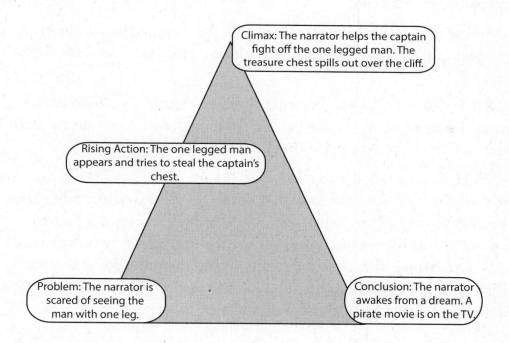

Climax: The narrator helps the captain fight off the one legged man. The treasure chest spills out over the cliff.

Rising Action: The one legged man appears and tries to steal the captain's chest.

Problem: The narrator is scared of seeing the man with one leg.

Conclusion: The narrator awakes from a dream. A pirate movie is on the TV.

Writing the Draft

When writing the draft, it is important to keep in mind the effect of language on the tone of the piece. To achieve a good score, the writer must maintain an effective style and use words to indicate tone. In completing a story like *Treasure Island*, it is important to understand the effect of language or tone, and therefore it is important to keep the tone of the story ending consistent with that of the author's writing. Note in the story on the next page how the tone stays consistent.

Sample Story Ending

But one day that one-legged man did come. I could hear very clearly the sound of the peg striking the cobblestone from down the road. Every other step, a knock of wood sounded against the stone. At first I tried to wish it to be something else, but I erased my fear and went to find the captain.

He was at his usual spot, standing at the cliff above the cove with his spy glass trained on the sea.

"Aye, good of you to come, Jim," the captain said.

"You told me to keep an eye for a one-legged man," I said. "I hear a peg leg coming up the road."

"An eye or an ear, no matter," said the captain, putting down his spy glass. "I had this looking the wrong way. Help me, Jim. Back to the Benbow."

We hurried back to the inn, but it was too late. As we entered the parlor, I saw a peg leg on the top stair. The captain moved faster than I had ever seen him move. "Me chest! Hurry with me, Jim!"

Not knowing what the captain expected me to do against the monster from my imaginings, I followed the captain as he bounded up the steps. The second floor of our quiet inn had four small rooms. We had put the captain in the room farthest down the hall by the back entrance so he could come and go without disturbing the other guests so much. This was to our great benefit now, for the peg leg was in the first room, rummaging about for a chest that was not there.

The captain bounded past that room without even glancing in. His eyes were locked on his door. He was in and out again with his sea chest before the peg leg appeared in the hallway.

"Captain!" I yelled as I saw something flash in the dim hallway.

"He's got his saber! Follow me, Jim, and be quick!"

Then the captain was gone, out the back entrance to the inn. I did not dare look back. Fear of the sword striking me propelled me forward, shoving me out and down the back stairs. The captain was already scurrying away from the inn, though the weight of the sea chest slowed him down.

"My chest!" the man called above me as his peg leg hit each step. "Come back here, boy!"

I ran. The captain was going back to his spot on the cliff. It was his only other spot. I caught up with him as he reached the edge, the sea swirling a hundred feet below.

"We've got to get away, Jim," the captain said.

"If we can get to town, we can get help," I said. "If we can get the Squire—"

"No time for help."

We both turned and saw the man with the peg leg emerge from trees. His sword hung at his side, the steel glinting in the sun. "My chest," he said.

"You won't have it," the captain said. "You can't have it."

"Fifteen men on a dead man's chest," the man sang. "I guess that man will be you."

The man stepped forward, and his sword came up to waist.

For the first time, I saw real fear in the captain's eyes. Without thinking, I jumped at the man's leg. He was unsteady on his feet, but he did not fall as I had hoped. He kicked me away, a stab of pain registering in my side, and he stumbled toward the captain, who remained planted at the cliff's edge.

As the sword raised high above the man's head, the captain lifted the sea chest above his to block the blow. I saw the sword strike the chest, a spark of metal on metal. Something slid away from the chest as the captain fell back, and the top of the chest broke open.

My eyes hurt as the silver and gold caught the sun. The captain tried reaching for something, but all he caught was the man's arm. The chest fell away, and its contents rained down the cliff.

"No!" the man called out, although I could not be certain whether it was after his gold or the way the captain brought him down. Both men spilled over the cliff's edge.

I leapt after them, catching the man's arm and seeing the captain clinging to the peg leg.

"Pull, Jim, pull!" the captain cried.

But I could not bring up both men. I did not even have the strength for one. Slowly I felt the fingers slipping from mine. . .

Just then an alarm buzzed. I opened my eyes. The TV was still on; I had forgotten to put the sleep setting on. On the screen, pirates fought over a familiar chest. "You can't have it!" a seafaring man with one leg called. "It's Jim's, I tell ya!"

Maybe I should have been a pirate.

Commentary

This Prose Constructed Response shows what is happening without ever giving away the ending. The story uses the elements of the reading (the captain, the man with one leg, the setting, and even the pirate song) in it, tying the two together like they were one story. The idea of it all being in the narrator's dream is clever, but it's not too much of a stretch to say that it has been done before. The response addresses the prompt and demonstrates purposeful coherence, clarity, and cohesion. It also establishes and maintains an effective style and demonstrates a command of the conventions of standard English. It scores a 4.

Narrative Writing Task #2—Describe a Historical Account

Directions: Today you will read the beginning of a historical account, related to the Battle of Yorktown. As you read, pay close attention to historical details and conflict as you prepare to complete a historical account.

By the summer of 1781, the United States had been at war with England for over six years. The first shots had been fired in April 1775 on the village green in Lexington and at North Bridge in Concord, Massachusetts. Merely sustaining the army had been a major accomplishment for the Americans, who did not have much money, food or clothing. The winters of 1777–78 at Valley Forge and 1779–80 at Morristown were particularly devastating, with many soldiers freezing and starving to death, and some giving up and returning home. A deep belief in the cause and an enduring faith in their leader, George Washington, kept this army together.

In the summer of 1780, the Americans received a major boost to their cause when 5,500 French troops, commanded by Comte de Rochambeau, arrived at Newport, Rhode Island. France had been sending supplies to the United States all along, but after France and England declared war against each other in 1778, French King Louis XVI sent troops and naval assistance to the United States to engage the enemy.

When Rochambeau's forces arrived, the British were operating on two fronts. General Clinton, commander of British forces in North America, was occupying New York City after a largely unsuccessful attempt to control the northern and middle colonies. General Lord Cornwallis was leading through the southern colonies an army that had already captured Savannah and Charleston. The main American army under Washington was stationed along the Hudson River above New York City.

In the spring of 1781, Washington traveled to Rhode Island to meet with Comte de Rochambeau and plan an attack on Clinton. A French fleet was expected to arrive in New York later that summer, and Washington wanted to coordinate the attack with the fleet's arrival. As planned, Rochambeau's army marched in July and joined with Washington's troops outside New York City, only to learn that the French fleet was sailing to the lower Chesapeake Bay.

Washington changed his strategy to make Clinton think he was planning to attack him, while instead sneaking away to the south to trap Cornwallis. In order to fool Clinton, Washington had his men build big army camps and huge brick bread ovens visible from New York to give the appearance of preparations for a stay. Washington also prepared false papers under his signature discussing plans for an attack on Clinton, and let these papers fall into British hands. Leaving a small force behind, Washington and Rochambeau set out for Yorktown in mid-August. By early September they were parading before the Continental Congress in Philadelphia, and they arrived in Williamsburg, 13 miles west of Yorktown, in mid September.

Cornwallis was in Yorktown because he had been ordered by Clinton during the summer to provide a protected harbor for the British fleet in the lower Chesapeake Bay. Cornwallis chose Yorktown because of its deep-water harbor on the York River. His army spent the latter part of the summer fortifying Yorktown and Gloucester Point across the York River.

The French fleet, as part of the overall plan, entered the lower Chesapeake Bay in the end of August and disembarked 3,000 French troops to wait for Washington and Rochambeau in Williamsburg. On September 5, they encountered the British fleet in a naval engagement known as the Battle of the Capes. The British suffered damage to their ships and returned to New York, while the French, commanded by Admiral de Grasse, remained in the lower Chesapeake and established a blockade.

By the end of September, approximately 17,600 American and French soldiers were gathered in Williamsburg, while 8,300 British soldiers were occupying Yorktown.

From "History of the Siege," National Park Service, http://www.nps.gov/york/history culture/history-of-the-siege.htm.

Time: 50 minutes

Directions: In the above passage, a historical account of the Siege of Yorktown is introduced. Think about the sequence of events that led to the Siege of Yorktown, and share these events in a well-written narrative description.

Complete this historical account, and discuss the series of events that led to the Siege of Yorktown. In your narrative, be sure to use accurate details from what you have learned about these events as you explain what happened both before and after.

Method #2: Using a Chart

Examine the planning chart that follows. Charting is a good technique to use if you prefer to write lists and then organize your thoughts based on the ideas you've jotted down.

 HELPFUL HINT

For PARCC, you should use any prior knowledge on the subject to help you complete your response. In other words, if you have learned about the subject, you can use the things you learned (not just what you read in the article) to add to your response. Prior knowledge only makes your writing better. Use it!

Notice that the questions who? what? when? where? why? and how? are all addressed in this prewriting chart. Now look at the sample essay that has been written from this prewriting.

- **Who?** The American army with help from the French against the British army and navy
- **What?** The defeat of the British and the end of the war
- **Where?** Yorktown, VA
- **When?** 1781
- **Why?** The French army and navy help the Americans surround the British. Cut off from escape, the army must surrender, and the war ends, giving America independence.

Sample

Although the first battles of the American Revolution went well, the British quickly gained the upper hand, defeating Washington's amateur army and chasing it around the colonies. However, Washington knew that if he could keep his army together, he could eventually wear out the will of the British to keep fighting.

The darkest days of the Revolution were in the winter of 1777–78 at Valley Forge, when Washington's army dwindled and those that remained struggled to survive. However, it did survive, and soon after, with the help of Benjamin Franklin, the Americans gained a valuable ally in France.

The French wanted revenge for losing Canada after the French and Indian War, and helping the American colonies was the way to do it. First, the French supplied weapons and ammunition to the Americans, and then the French army and navy came to fight alongside the Americans.

In 1781, the British army marched south to Virginia, where it was protected on one side by the British navy. However, the French navy from the Caribbean sailed north and defeated the British navy, cutting off the British army's escape route. Then a combined American and French army marched south and surrounded the British army at Yorktown. After a series of bombardments, and with no chance of escape, General Cornwallis surrendered his army.

With the surrender, the British had no large army in America anymore. It would have been difficult to send another army and another navy to protect it just to resume fighting. But the British had had enough. With Corwallis's surrender, the American Revolution effectively ended, although the Treaty of Paris would not be signed until 1783. Washington had kept his army together and, in doing so, had defeated the most powerful nation in the world.

Commentary

This writer approached the task using both the prompt and his knowledge of the Revolutionary War to create an effective Prose Constructed Response. The use of many specific details (like referring to French defeat in the French and Indian War as France's motivation to aid the Americans) helps make this a strong PCR. The writer uses both the prompt and his knowledge to expand this narrative into an informative narrative description. The response provides comprehensive development of the topic using convincing reasoning and details while maintaining an effective style and while following the conventions of standard English. It scores a 4.

Narrative Writing Task #3—Describe a Scientific Process

Read the beginning of a scientific process, related to the life cycle of a frog. As you read, pay close attention to scientific details as you prepare to complete the scientific process.

The life of a frog begins as an egg. Frogs mate usually in water. Female frogs lay their fertilized eggs in water or in wet places, and most of the time, the eggs are laid among vegetation. The vegetation provides protection for the eggs, hiding the mass from hungry predators. Most species of frog lay their eggs in one mass, and most, but not all, species of frog leave the egg masses (called spawn) to develop on their own.

Some of these eggs will die or be eaten by predators, but most will start a long journey to adulthood. First the egg yolk splits into two cells, and then it splits again in two, making four cells, and again it splits and again it splits, each time adding new cells growing inside the egg. Slowly, each egg changes from just a jelly-like sac into something resembling a tadpole inside the egg. After about three weeks, depending on the species, the egg is ready for the next phase of the frog life cycle.

That egg must change and change again before it turns into an adult frog.

Time: 50 minutes

Directions: In the above passage, a scientific process of the life cycle of a frog is introduced. Think about the sequence of events that occur after the egg phase and share the following phases in a well-written, logically organized narrative description. Complete this scientific process, and discuss the consecutive phases. In your narrative, be sure to use accurate facts from what you have learned about these phases, noting the role of the phases that occur after the new crescent as you explain what happens next.

Method #3: Using a Graphic Organizer

Graphic organizers and flow charts help writers to unpack meaning and answer questions before they begin writing. During each step, the writer is able to think on paper. Fill in the graphic organizer that follows, based on the prompt for Narrative Writing Task #3.

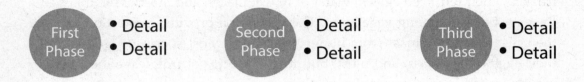

First Phase
• Detail
• Detail

Second Phase
• Detail
• Detail

Third Phase
• Detail
• Detail

 HELPFUL HINT

Note that you can and should use prior knowledge when you are making your response. It will give your response more detail, and the detail will be more accurate.

Each idea in your graphic organizer should lead to an extension or further development. In this exercise, you are thinking of the process sequentially. Look at the sample essay below and the prewriting graphic organizer that precedes it. Can you see the connections between the graphic organizer and the essay?

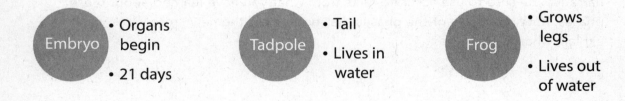

Embryo
• Organs begin
• 21 days

Tadpole
• Tail
• Lives in water

Frog
• Grows legs
• Lives out of water

Sample

A frog begins as an egg that is laid in water. That egg has to change three times before it becomes an adult frog. Each change is very different. Each stage looks like a different creature instead of one single organism.

Once it is no longer an egg, the frog becomes an embryo. The embryo lives on its egg sac. It is at this phase that the organs of the frog begin to develop. This stage lasts about twenty one days before becoming the next phase of the frog life cycle.

The embryo changes until it is what is called a tadpole. The tadpole looks more like a fish than a frog because of its long tail. It needs this tail because it lives completely in water, breathing through gills. The tadpole uses its underwater environment for protection and cover so that it can continue to grow until its final phase.

At the end of the tadpole stage, the frog begins to grow hind legs. The tadpole stops using gills and starts breathing air through lungs. When the tadpole's tail is gone and legs are in its place, it has become an adult frog.

The frog's life cycle is more than just a smaller version of itself, constantly growing until adulthood, like humans and other animals. Instead, the frog goes through very distinct phases that are unlike the others. The process is not complete until the frog hops onto land as an adult and then lays eggs to start the next life cycle.

Commentary

This writer approached the task using writing skills and scientific knowledge to create an effective Prose Constructed Response. Again, the use of many specific details (tail, gills, hind legs, and breathing air) all help make this a strong PCR. This narrative description starts and ends well, with the reference to the egg at the beginning to the laying the next generation's eggs in the conclusion. The response has a logical progression of ideas, and the development is appropriate to the task, purpose, and audience. It scores a 4.

CHAPTER REVIEW

> Plan and prewrite before you write your Prose Constructed Response, using any of the formats shown in this chapter. Even though you are not graded on your prewriting, three to five minutes of planning will pay off when you write your essay. You will not score as well as you could if you do not plan.

> Whatever method of prewriting you choose, make sure that you use a clear method of organization that works best for you.

> When completing a story, show, don't tell, what is happening. Let the reader figure things out.

> Try for compositional risk. Try something different. Think outside the box to make a story that is beyond the ordinary.

> When completing a story, be sure to use the characters, setting, and style of the reading. Your PCR should be creative but still be a completion of what you have read.

> When describing a historical event or a scientific process, use what you have learned in (and out of) school. Do not rely on the prompt alone.

> In historical and scientific PCRs, the more details you include, the better.

The Literary Analysis Task

CHAPTER 4

Comparing and Contrasting Two Texts

The Literary Analysis Task goes beyond asking questions about a text. It even goes beyond requiring students to write an essay about a text. Instead, the challenge of the Literary Analysis Task is to require students to both answer questions and then write an essay about *two* texts.

Students will be given 80 minutes to complete the Literary Analysis Task. In the past, students were tasked with writing a persuasive essay on a common (usually school-related) topic. With PARCC, students will have to read a combination of two essays, stories, poems, or narratives and then write an essay showing a deep understanding of both.

Basically, students will have to write a compare and contrast essay about the two texts after answering the reading questions for both. So what is the best approach to this challenge?

Before You Read

Before you can write a compare and contrast essay, it is important to *gather information as you read*. You can use either a Venn diagram or a simple T-chart to jot down notes on what you are reading. They are two good ways of gathering ideas, although there are, of course, many others.

As a quick refresher, a Venn diagram looks like this:

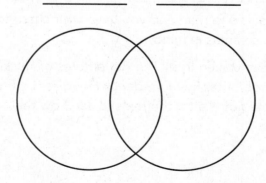

A T-chart looks like this:

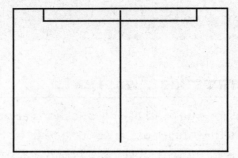

As you read and take notes on your Venn diagram or T-chart, look at these areas to find similarities and differences:

- titles,
- author,
- plot (What are the two texts about),
- author's tone or mood,
- imagery,
- the form or narration of the story,
- setting,
- theme,
- characters,
- words that are symbols or are repeated,
- similes or metaphors,
- patterns in words or phrases,
- dialect or slang.

As You Read

Now that you have prepared to read and you have your chart, take notes on the texts as you read keeping those areas in mind.

Read the following texts, taken from *The Adventures of Huckleberry Finn* by Mark Twain and from *The Autobiography of Frederick Douglass* by Frederick Douglass. Then look at the example notes after the texts to see how they compare and contrast.

From chapter five of *The Adventures of Huckleberry Finn* by Mark Twain:

He was at most fifty, and he looked it. His hair was long and tangled and greasy, and hung down, and you could see his eyes shining through like he was behind vines. It was all black, no gray; so was his long, mixed-up whiskers. There warn't no color in his face, where his face showed; it was white; not like another man's white, but a white to make a body sick, a white to make a body's flesh crawl—a tree-toad white, a fish-belly white. As for his clothes—just rags, that was all. He had one ankle resting on t'other knee; the boot on that foot was busted, and two of his toes stuck through, and he worked them now and then. His hat was laying on the floor—an old black slouch with the top caved in, like a lid.

I stood a-looking at him; he set there a-looking at me, with his chair tilted back a little. I set the candle down. I noticed the window was up; so he had clumb in by the shed. He kept a-looking me all over. By and by he says:

"Starchy clothes—very. You think you're a good deal of a big-bug, *don't* you?"

"Maybe I am, maybe I ain't," I says.

"Don't you give me none o' your lip," says he. "You've put on considerable many frills since I been away. I'll take you down a peg before I get done with you. You're educated, too, they say—can read and write. You think you're better'n your father, now, don't you, because he can't? *I'll* take it out of you. Who told you you might meddle with such hifalut'n foolishness, hey?—who told you you could?"

"The widow. She told me."

"The widow, hey?—and who told the widow she could put in her shovel about a thing that ain't none of her business?"

"Nobody never told her."

"Well, I'll learn her how to meddle. And looky here—you drop that school, you hear? I'll learn people to bring up a boy to put on airs over his own father and let on to be better'n what *he* is. You lemme catch you fooling around that school again, you hear? Your mother couldn't read, and she couldn't write, nuther, before she died. None of the family couldn't before *they* died. I can't; and here you're aswelling yourself up like this. I ain't the man to stand it—you hear? Say, lemme hear you read."

I took up a book and begun something about General Washington and the wars. When I'd read about a half a minute, he fetched the book a whack with his hand and knocked it across the house. He says:

"It's so. You can do it. I had my doubts when you told me. Now looky here; you stop that putting on frills. I won't have it. I'll lay for you, my smarty; and if I catch you about that school I'll tan you good. First you know you'll get religion, too. I never see such a son."

He took up a little blue and yaller picture of some cows and a boy, and says:

"What's this?"

"It's something they give me for learning my lessons good."

He tore it up, and says:

"I'll give you something better—I'll give you a cowhide."

He set there a-mumbling and a-growling a minute, and then he says:

"*Ain't* you a sweet-scented dandy, though? A bed; and bedclothes; and a look'n'glass; and a piece of carpet on the floor—and your own father got to sleep with the hogs in the tanyard. I never see such a son. I bet I'll take some o' these frills out o' you before I'm done with you. Why, there ain't no end to your airs—they say you're rich. Hey?—how's that?"

"They lie—that's how."

"Looky here—mind how you talk to me; I'm a-standing about all I can stand now—so don't gimme no sass. I've been in town two days, and I hain't heard nothing but about you bein' rich. I heard about it away down the river, too. That's why I come. You git me that money to-morrow—I want it."

"I hain't got no money."

"It's a lie. Judge Thatcher's got it. You git it. I want it."

"I hain't got no money, I tell you. You ask Judge Thatcher; he'll tell you the same."

"All right. I'll ask him; and I'll make him pungle, too, or I'll know the reason why. Say, how much you got in your pocket? I want it."

"I hain't got only a dollar, and I want that to—"

"It don't make no difference what you want it for—you just shell it out."

From chapter seven of *The Autobiography of Frederick Douglass*:

I lived in Master Hugh's family about seven years. During this time, I succeeded in learning to read and write. In accomplishing this, I was compelled to resort to various stratagems. I had no regular teacher. My mistress, who had kindly commenced to instruct me, had, in compliance with the advice and direction of her husband, not only ceased to instruct, but had set her face against my being instructed by any one else. It is due, however, to my mistress to say of her, that she did not adopt this course of treatment immediately. She at first lacked the depravity indispensable to shutting me up in mental darkness. It was at least necessary for her to have some training in the exercise of irresponsible power, to make her equal to the task of treating me as though I were a brute.

My mistress was, as I have said, a kind and tender-hearted woman; and in the simplicity of her soul she commenced, when I first went to live with her, to treat me as she supposed one human being ought to treat another. In entering upon the duties of a slaveholder, she did not seem to perceive that I sustained to her the relation of a mere chattel, and that for her to treat me as a human being was not only wrong, but dangerously so. Slavery proved as injurious to her as it did to me. When I went there, she was a pious, warm, and tender-hearted woman. There was no sorrow or suffering for which she had not a tear. She had bread for the hungry, clothes for the naked, and comfort for every mourner that came within her reach. Slavery soon proved its ability to divest her of these heavenly qualities. Under its influence, the tender heart became stone, and the lamblike disposition gave way to one of tiger-like fierceness. The first step in her downward course was in her ceasing to instruct me. She now commenced to practice her husband's precepts. She finally became even more violent in her opposition than her husband himself. She was not satisfied with simply doing as well as he had commanded; she seemed anxious to do better. Nothing seemed to make her more angry than to see me with a newspaper. She seemed to think that here lay the danger. I have had her rush at me with a face made all up of fury, and snatch from me a newspaper, in a manner that fully revealed her apprehension. She was an apt woman; and a little experience soon demonstrated, to her satisfaction, that education and slavery were incompatible with each other.

From this time I was most narrowly watched. If I was in a separate room any considerable length of time, I was sure to be suspected of having a book, and was at once called to give an account of myself. All this, however, was too late. The first step had been taken. Mistress, in teaching me the alphabet, had given me the *inch,* and no precaution could prevent me from taking the *ell.*

The plan which I adopted, and the one by which I was most successful, was that of making friends of all the little white boys whom I met in the street. As many of these as I could, I converted into teachers. With their kindly aid, obtained at different times and in different places, I finally succeeded in learning to read. When I was sent of errands, I always took my book with me, and by going one part of my errand quickly, I found time to get a lesson before my return. I used also to carry bread with me, enough of which was always in the house, and to which I was always welcome; for I was much better off in this regard than many of the poor white children in our neighborhood. This bread I used to bestow upon the hungry little urchins, who, in return, would give me that more valuable bread of knowledge. I am strongly tempted to give the names of two or three of those little boys, as a testimonial of the gratitude and affection I bear them; but prudence forbids;—not that it would injure me, but it might embarrass them; for it is almost an unpardonable offence to teach slaves to read in this Christian country. It is enough to say of the dear little fellows, that they lived on Philpot Street, very near Durgin and Bailey's ship-yard. I used to talk this matter of slavery over with them. I would sometimes say to them, I wished I could be as free as they would be when they got to be men. "You will be free as soon as you are twenty-one, *but I am a slave for life!* Have not I as good a right to be free as you have?" These words used to trouble them; they would express for me the liveliest sympathy, and console me with the hope that something would occur by which I might be free.

I was now about twelve years old, and the thought of being *a slave for life* began to bear heavily upon my heart. Just about this time, I got hold of a book entitled "The Columbian Orator." Every opportunity I got, I used to read this book. Among much of other interesting matter, I found in it a dialogue between a master and his slave. The slave was represented as having run away from his master three times. The dialogue represented the conversation which took place between them, when the slave was retaken the third time. In this dialogue, the whole argument in behalf of slavery was brought forward by the master, all of which was disposed of by the slave. The slave was made to say some very smart as well as impressive things in reply to his master—things which had the desired though unexpected effect; for the conversation resulted in the voluntary emancipation of the slave on the part of the master.

Now look at the notes taken for the texts:

Huckleberry Finn

Author: Mark Twain

Setting: 1800s in the South

Plot: Getting an education—Dad found out—threatened to beat him

Character: Huck doesn't protest when Dad tells him to stop learning, but he does when Dad demands money. Huck's Dad doesn't want Huck to learn because he'll be "better" than he is.

Theme: Huck does not seem to care whether he is educated or not. He only fears his father.

Literary Devices: The use of slang.

Tone: Light and humorous even though the Dad is threatening his son.

Patterns: His Dad threatens to beat him and doesn't want him to be better.

Words as Symbols: None

Dialect: Characters talk with strong Southern accents and use a lot of slang.

Frederick Douglass

Author: Frederick Douglass

Setting: 1800s (pre-Civil War) in the South

Plot: Getting an education—master found out—wasn't allowed

Characterization: After the mistress of the house had started to teach him how to read, Master Hugh stopped her, and Douglass had to sneak books to teach himself.

Theme: Douglass sees learning as his hope, and he learns to want freedom from it.

Literary Devices: Use of proper English.

Tone: Serious. Douglass is a slave who wants to learn and be free.

Patterns: The master and mistress both are strict and try to keep Douglass from learning and being better.

Words as Symbols: None

Dialect: Even though he must be in the South, Douglass's narration uses proper English with no slang.

After You Read

Once you have finished reading and taking your notes on both texts, read the essay topic and then organize your prewriting and make your outline. Look at the essay topic for these texts:

Directions: In *The Adventures of Huckleberry Finn* and *The Autobiography of Frederick Douglass*, the authors express different ideas about getting an education. Write an essay that analyzes the authors' views on what education is and what it can do for people. Remember to use details from both texts to support your ideas.

Now review the notes you have taken. Ask yourself:

- What similarities are there?
- What differences are there?
- Are there other areas that would help the essay?
- What areas have nothing that would help a compare and contrast essay?

As you think about the similarities and differences, underline or highlight the ones that are important. Let's look at what to underline from this prewriting in T chart form.

Huckleberry Finn	Topics in My Notes	Frederick Douglass
Mark Twain	**Author**	Frederick Douglass
1800s in the South	**Setting**	1800s (pre-Civil War) in the South
Getting an education—Dad found out—threatened to beat him	**Plot**	Getting an education—master found out—wasn't allowed
Huck doesn't protest when Dad tells him to stop learning, but he does when Dad demands money. Huck's Dad doesn't want Huck to learn because he'll be "better" than he is.	**Characterization**	After the mistress of the house had started to teach him how to read, Master Hugh stopped her, and Douglass had to sneak books to teach himself.
Huck does not seem to care whether he is educated or not. He only fears his father.	**Theme**	Douglass sees learning as his hope, and he learns to want freedom from it.

Huckleberry Finn	Topics in My Notes	Frederick Douglass
Use of Slang	**Literary Devices**	Use of proper English
Light and humorous even though the Dad is threatening his son.	**Tone**	Serious. Douglass is a slave who wants to learn and be free.
His Dad threatens to beat him and doesn't want him to be better.	**Patterns**	The master and mistress both are strict and try to keep Douglass from learning and being better.
None	**Words as Symbols**	None
Characters talk with strong Southern accents and use a lot of slang	**Dialect**	Even though he must be in the South, Douglass's narration uses proper English with no slang.
Very good	**Quality**	Very good

Once you have identified the important similarities and differences, make your outline. Start with your claim since that will be what you are trying to prove. Think of it like a topic sentence for the whole essay.

Here is a formula that every claim has:

The Topic + Your Opinion = Claim

Some people include the reasons in the the claim. If you do, make sure that you put them in the order in which they will appear.

 HELPFUL HINT

Generally, you should not use "I" or "me" or "my," such as "I think that...." The claim is about the topic, not about you.

For example, here are two claims for the topic:

- Although both *Huckleberry Finn* and *The Autobiography of Frederick Douglass* have similarities about what happens when the main character starts to get an education, their tones and themes about education are strikingly different.
- The passages from *Huckleberry Finn* and *The Autobiography of Frederick Douglass* are about the roadblocks for Southern boys to get an education, but *Huckleberry Finn* sees learning as something all in good fun while *Frederick Douglass* sees it as terribly important.

The Outline

Once you've brainstormed ideas and written your claim, the next step is to organize your ideas. In a compare and contrast essay, one method of organizing ideas is using order of importance for your ideas. Order of importance puts your reasons in order from weakest to strongest. This helps to build your argument and advance your ideas.

Look back at what you underlined. See if you can group anything together. Have your strongest support at the end of the essay. It should go something like this:

- Similarities: Both stories have adults who try to stop the kids from learning.
- Difference: Huck Finn is lighter in tone—education is not as important.
- Difference: Frederick Douglass is serious—education means a path to freedom.

Paragraph 1 will be the intro, ending with the claim.

 **HELPFUL HINT**

It usually is easier to save planning the introduction until after you have planned the rest of the essay.

Here is a quick plan for an introduction outline:

- Hook.
- Central Idea.
- Claim.

Paragraph 5 will be the conclusion. Here is a simple way to plan a conclusion:

- *Restate* (don't copy) the claim.
- Summarize the first reason (paragraph 2).
- Summarize the second reason (paragraph 3).
- Summarize the third reason (paragraph 4).
- Strong closing statement. (Demand what you want!)

One more thing: As you are making your outline, pull pieces of the text (called *evidence* or *citations*) that you see to help support your paper. Using specific evidence from the text (the author's own words) is the best evidence you can provide in an essay. *Be sure to surround the author's words with quotation marks to show that they are from that author and not your own words!*

So here is a sample outline for this essay (note the quotes taken from the texts):

I. Introduction

    A. Both HF and FD are American classics.

    B. Written in same time period.

    C. Before the Civil War in the South.

    D. Two boys are stopped from learning to read.

    E. Although both *Huckleberry Finn* and *the Autobiography of Frederick Douglass* have similarities about what happens when the main character starts to get an education, their tones and themes about education are strikingly different.

II. Similarities

    A. Set in pre-Civil War South—HF is poor and FD is a slave.

    B. After adult found out about learning, tried to stop him.

        1. "And looky here—you drop that school, you hear?"

    C. Both Master and Dad are strict and try to stop the boys.

        1. "My mistress, who had kindly commenced to instruct me, had, in compliance with the advice and direction of her husband, not only ceased to instruct, but had set her face against my being instructed by any one else."

    D. Both don't want boys to be "better."

III. HF Lighter Tone

    A. Dad is violent and constantly threatens Huck.

        1. "if I catch you about that school I'll tan you good"

    B. Even though Huck knows Dad is violent, when Dad questions him about having money, Huck says, "They lie—that's how."

    C. Mark Twain sets a lighter tone. Dad is dangerous, but he's a comic character.

        1. "He set there a-mumbling and a-growling a minute."

    D. Uses dialect and accents to set the lighter tone.

IV. FD Serious Tone

    A. FD had been taught by the Mistress of the house, but "Slavery proved as injurious to her as it did to me."

        1. She changed and became worse than her husband.

    B. He was not allowed to read.

        1. "Education and slavery were incompatible with each other."

    C. She feared exactly what happened for Douglass. He read a book about a slave who ran away.

        1. "the whole argument in behalf of slavery was brought forward by the master, all of which was disposed of by the slave."

        2. Douglass learned to want freedom from reading.

    D. There is no dialect. The proper English helps set a serious tone.

V. Conclusion

    A. While similar, HF and FD have different attitudes toward education.

    B. Both have people trying to stop the main character from learning.

    C. HF doesn't seem to care, and the whole scene is meant to be funny.

    D. FD cares deeply. Slavery and reading change his mistress for the worse, and it makes him want freedom.

    E. From reading these texts, we can learn that reading sets us free.

Writing the Essay

After you have written the outline, you have reached the easy point (believe it or not)! When you write, **follow your outline.** If you follow your outline, you will have a strong paper. It's small things now. Keep good grammar and sentence writing in mind.

Sample Essay

June to September never seems long enough. In August, millions of American children moan when they hear television commercials advertise "back-to-school" deals; yet, by the time September arrives, these same children find themselves in class, happily chatting with friends, eagerly looking at the fresh new textbooks for the year. It seems that many Americans take for granted the simple fact that, unlike some countries, we are fortunate enough to get to go to school every year. A much different attitude about education is portrayed in two American classics, "Huckleberry Finn" and "The Autobiography of Frederick Douglass." Although both "Huckleberry Finn" and "The Autobiography of Frederick Douglass" have similarities about what happens when the main character starts to get an education, their tones and themes about education are strikingly different.

Even though there are many differences in these two texts, the two books share many characteristics. The setting for both stories is the same; both are set in the South before the Civil War. In this society, there is a definite class system, which is depicted in both texts. The adults who try to prevent Huck and Douglass from becoming educated view an education as a way to rise above their current position. Huck's father says to him, "And looky here—you drop that school, you hear?" Douglass notes, "My mistress, who had kindly commenced to instruct me, had, in compliance with the advice and direction of her husband, not only ceased to instruct, but had set her face against my being instructed by any one else."

The tones that the authors set in the two pieces are very different, and this can be seen in the interactions that the characters have with each other. By using dialect, Twain's text is presented with some humor mixed in. Twain creates the image of Huck's father as a man who is introduced as greasy, hairy, and dirty with sickly white skin; he seems almost comical with toes pointing out of his boots. The father's constant threats to Huck, "if I catch you about that school I'll tan you good," are intermingled with Huck's observations of his father, "He set there a-mumbling and a-growling a minute." Huck shows the reader how intelligent he actually is when he tells his father he doesn't have any money. When his father asks why everyone says Huck has money, Huck responds, "They lie that's how." Huck realizes that his dad taking all of his money would be much worse than a beating.

Douglass demonstrates how intelligent he is by seeking out opportunities to be taught to read. He barters with white boys: bread for education. Unlike Twain, Douglass does not use dialect or humor to convey his message. The vocabulary that he chooses creates an image of someone who has worked hard to learn and use challenging words. He is appealing to an educated audience in an attempt to show that slaves are human and should be taught to read. He explains that in order for masters to view slaves as nonhuman (chattel or brutes), they could not allow their slaves to read. He explains how practicing this made the master's wife a bitter person, and comes to the conclusion, "Education and slavery were incompatible with each other."

It is clear that both of these boys are intelligent, but they demonstrate their intelligence differently. Huck does not really seem to care about school, but he shows how smart he is by protecting his money from his father. Douglass cannot go to school but realizes that education is a path to freedom and finds any opportunity to pursue it, even if it makes his master angry. It is truly sad that the adults depicted in these selections are shown as people who try to prevent children from receiving an education because they didn't want these boys to be "better" than what they were. However, Huck and Douglass are smart enough to realize that reading has set them both free from the ignorance around them, which is an important lesson for us all: reading sets us free.

Commentary

The response has a comprehensive development of the topic using convincing text-based evidence. It has a strong introduction, conclusion, and progression of ideas. The response demonstrates a command of standard English. It scores a 4.

When you proofread, insert some great transitions to make your essay flow:

Compare	Contrast
also	although
as	but
as well	even though
both	however
like	in contrast
likewise	instead
mostly	nevertheless
same	on the contrary
similarly	on the other hand
the same as	unlike
too	while
	yet

CHAPTER REVIEW

> When you create a T-chart, be sure that you are collecting information on the same characteristics of both texts.

> Part of the evidence is the source of the text. Consider when the text was written and what website published it. In this case, one of the points we were able to make was that the settings of the stories were similar.

The Research Simulation Task

Write a Mini Research Paper

One day, your teacher announces that you are going to write a research paper. She tells you that you can choose any topic you like, that you are going to go to the library for a week to conduct the research, and that you have to cite at least two different sources on your topic. Your mind races with all of the different topics that you could research, and eventually, you determine your topic and begin the process of sifting through Internet sites, books, magazine articles, videos, and pictures so that you can begin writing your essay. You take careful notes from your sources, you reference direct quotes with quotation marks and a reference to the pages on which you found the information, and, as you watch a video, you write down the time that the speaker makes that point that reinforces your thesis statement. You write a first draft, revise it, produce a final draft, and place your well-written, cited paper into your teacher's hands on the due date.

Baseball at Night by Morris Kantor (1934)
Smithsonian American Art Museum
Gift of Mrs. Morris Kantor

83

The Research Simulation Task on the PARCC exam is designed to mimic this entire process in the span of 85 minutes. The good news is this: the makers of the PARCC exam have already conducted the research for you. All you have to do is read it and determine what information will help you write the best essay in the time allotted.

When we said, "your teacher" in the scenario above, you may have pictured your English teacher assigning you this project after the class finished reading a book. This is not the case on the PARCC exam. The Research Simulation Task is designed to incorporate all subject areas.

Because this portion of the exam involves all subjects, you can easily practice the skills of synthesizing and analyzing information all year long with things that you already enjoy. Here is the key: read at least one piece of nonfiction, one piece of fiction (including poetry), and watch a video or view a picture or art in that subject. For example, if you like baseball, try:

Nonfiction	Fiction	Video
Read an account of last night's game	*Shoeless Joe* by W.P. Kinsella	Watch an analysis by a sportscaster
A Nice Little Place on the North Side by George Will	*The Natural* by Bernard Malamud	Watch an interpretation of one of the pieces of fiction

In addition to nonfiction, fiction, video, photographs, and art, you may have to interpret a chart. Staying with the example of baseball, the PARCC may ask you to use the following chart as a source of evidence in conjunction with a video about players from the early days of baseball.

Player	Seasons Played	Years Played	Games Played	Batting Average	Homeruns
Joe Jackson	13	1908–1920	1,330	0.356	54
Babe Ruth	22	1913–1935	2,503	0.342	46
Ty Cobb	24	1905–1928	3,034	0.366	117

Data compiled from the players' sites on www.baseball-reference.com

Like the other sections of the exam, you will read and answer questions upon the articles and media that you view. These questions can help you in responding to the essay at the end of the section. Remember that you have only 85 minutes to work on the entire section, so pay attention, take notes, and plan your time wisely.

Read the Directions

Each section of the PARCC exam will begin with directions that are in bold print. Please read them. They tell you the topic, what sources you will be reading, and what type of essay you will write. Knowing this information will help you manage your time as you take the test. As you read the directions, you can make a prediction as to what types of evidence you should look for as you progress through this section of the test. Using some of the baseball references above, here is a sample of what the directions may look like:

Directions: In 1919, the Chicago White Sox were accused of throwing the World Series. "Shoeless" Joe Jackson, a member of that team, was banned from baseball after a judge and jury found him not guilty of participating in the scandal.

Today, you will read two texts and view a short video about the World Series and "Shoeless" Joe. After you read, you will write an essay that analyzes the strength of the arguments the authors make about "Shoeless" Joe Jackson's involvement in the 1919 World Series scandal.

The first step in planning is considering these directions. Here are questions that you should ask and answer before you go to Question One, Part A.

What is the topic?	Shoeless Joe's involvement in the 1919 World Series
What sources will you use?	Two texts and a video
What type of essay will you write?	An analysis of the strength of the authors' arguments about Shoeless Joe's involvement
What evidence will you need?	My prediction is that one of the authors will say that he is innocent; another might claim that he did not do anything in the scandal but maybe knew something about it. I should look for what evidence is presented about his involvement.

Here is another sample set of directions:

> **Directions:** The route used to transport slaves from Africa to the Americas was called the Middle Passage. Because the conditions upon the ships that carried slaves were deplorable, antislavery activists cited the treatment of slaves on the Middle Passage as one of the primary reasons to abolish slavery.
>
> Today, you will learn about the Middle Passage by reading two texts, a bar graph, and a painting. One of the texts is an African-American folk tale; the second is an excerpt from an autobiography. When you are finished reading, you will write an essay that analyzes the strength of the arguments the authors make about the abolition of slavery.

What is the topic?	the abolition of slavery
What sources will you use?	A folktale, an autobiography, a bar graph, a painting
What type of essay will you write?	An analysis of the strength of the authors' arguments about abolition
What evidence will you need?	I should look for what kinds of appeals the authors make about getting rid of slavery. The directions say that the Middle Passage is one of the major reasons, I should carefully examine evidence presented on it.

Use the Questions on the Test to Gather Information

You have taken the time to read the directions and determine what you are looking for. Fortunately for you, the PARCC assists you in answering the essay question with the other questions on the test. As you work through this section, you are going to take notice of what the texts questions ask.

In the reading comprehension chapter, we discussed the format of the questions. Most of the questions ask specifically about a part of the text and then ask you to support your response from the first section. To illustrate this, here is a reprint of the questions from the practice with "Children in the Workhouses."

Part A

Which sentence explains how paragraph 3 is important to the development of the ideas in "Children in the Workhouses"?

Part B

Which quotation from paragraph 3 best supports the response to Part A?

Because you have to return to the text to find the answer, you are going reread. You should notice some evidence that you might use in your written response. When you find evidence that you think you may need later, write down the source and the paragraph in which you found the information and jot an idea or two.

You cannot copy and paste directly from the text into your essay, but you can navigate through the texts. You have the source and the paragraph as a guide, so tab to it as you write. The tabs will look like this:

Source B	Source C

Source A

In this case, Source A is the "active" document. You can switch to Sources B or C by clicking on the tab that you want.

You might think that citing information from a text is easier than citing information from a video or a picture. There is an easy way to cite information from a video: by the time. As you watch the video, place the pointer on the timer at the bottom of the video. When you hear something that you think you will need, record the time that it is said and jot down the idea. You do not have to jot what is said verbatim, or word for word, but you can get a general idea down with the specific time.

Again, it is helpful to use the questions on the video. As you answer these questions, the test will provide the specific time and the exact quote. These might just be what you are looking for.

There is no limit to how many times you watch a video, but there is a time limit for you to complete this section. Before you watch, check how long the video is. Most are two to three minutes long. If you watch the video twice, once for content and once for specific notes, you have spent six minutes. A better strategy is to read the questions first, pay special attention to where most of the responses fall, and then watch the video with the purpose of gathering notes. This should save you a couple of minutes.

For photographs or paintings, be specific about what you see and where you see it. Use phrases like, "In the upper right hand corner of the painting," "Across the bottom of the photograph," and "Below the woman's arm."

Look at the two sentences below that describe *Baseball at Night*, the painting featured at the beginning of the chapter. It is reproduced here for your reference:

Baseball at Night by Morris Kantor (1934)
Smithsonian American Art Museum
Gift of Mrs. Morris Kantor

NO: There is a group of men gathered in the picture.

YES: Just below the center of the painting, three men in baseball uniforms are gathered around first base while the umpire, situated to the lower right of them, looks on.

Remember that the title of the work and the context of where the information has been obtained are important, too. You can use this information as part of your evidence. This might be especially helpful if the sources you are viewing are from different eras. This painting is from the Smithsonian American Art Museum, was created in 1934 by Morris Kantor, and was titled *Baseball at Night*. Using that information, you might put in your essay, "During the Great Depression, one choice for nighttime entertainment was going to a baseball game."

Read the Essay Question Carefully

When you have finished answering all of the other questions, you will arrive at the essay. Fortunately, the directions will remain at the top of the screen as you navigate through the texts, and you will notice that they are very close to what the essay question will ask of you. Here is a sample of the directions for the essay:

Directions: You have read an excerpt from a book and an article, and watched a video describing "Shoeless" Joe Jackson and the 1919 World Series scandal. All three sources contain information that supports the claim that Jackson was an honest player. Carefully consider the argument each author uses to demonstrate Jackson's lack of involvement in the scandal. Write an essay that analyzes the strength of the arguments related to Jackson's innocence in at least two of the three supporting materials. Remember to use textual evidence to support your ideas.

Confirm what you need to do:

1. Write an essay that analyzes strength of arguments.
2. Use at least two of the three sources of information.
3. Use textual evidence to support what you say.

Notice that the question does NOT ask you to determine which article is the best. You are NOT ASKED to say, "Source One is the best because it makes the most sense, and the arguments are the strongest."

Instead, you are asked which *argument* is the strongest. This means that the authors probably used the same or similar arguments in their writing. You should look for which ones, out of all of the arguments made, have the most convincing points.

Aside from being asked to determine the strongest argument, you may be asked to explain a phenomenon or synthesize information across the texts. In these cases, you may see:

Directions: You have read an excerpt from a book and an article, watched a video describing "Shoeless" Joe Jackson and the 1919 World Series scandal, and examined a painting of a baseball game. All four sources contain depictions of baseball as a part of American culture. Carefully consider how baseball influences Americans. Using at least three of the four sources, write an essay that explains how baseball is part of American culture. Remember to use textual evidence to support your ideas.

In this case, you are asked to EXPLAIN how baseball is a part of American culture. Obviously, for this example, the directions would be different and might discuss the relationship that Americans have with baseball. Again, you are NOT asked to rank which source was the best, so you are NOT going to say, "Author One has the best ideas about baseball and Americans." You will look for similarities across the research provided and work with them.

Plan to Write the Essay

Before we go any further, we should take a moment to examine what the readers are expecting to see in your performance. You can review the draft PARCC rubric for writing at *http://www.parcconline.org/sites/parcc/files/Grade6-11-ELACondensed RubricFORANALYTICANDNARRATIVEWRITING.pdf.*

The rubric is on a 1–4 scale. For the sake of brevity, and because we expect the best of ourselves, we are going to examine what the characteristics of a 4 are for each category.

Characteristic	What PARCC Says	What This Means For You
Reading Comprehension of Key Ideas and Details	The student response provides an accurate analysis of what the text says explicitly and inferentially and cites convincing textual evidence to support the analysis, showing full comprehension of complex ideas expressed in the text(s).	You have actually read and understood the texts provided. You know which details are important for your argument and have cited them in your writing.
Written Expression: Logic	The student response addresses the prompt and provides effective and comprehensive development of the claim, topic, and/or narrative elements by using clear and convincing reasoning, details, text-based evidence, and/ or description; the development is consistently appropriate to the task, purpose, and audience.	If you don't understand what is asked of you and write something off topic, you will not receive credit. Throughout your essay, you use logic, appropriate details, and evidence that you did not create. You are not writing a text message to your friend; your writing reflects that you understand that your audience is comprised of very serious adults.

Characteristic	What PARCC Says	What This Means For You
Written Expression: Organization	The student response demonstrates purposeful coherence, clarity, and cohesion and includes a strong introduction, conclusion, and a logical, well-executed progression of ideas, making it easy to follow the writer's progression of ideas.	You have a well-organized essay that has the "good ingredients" of an introduction, a thesis, a body, and a conclusion. Additionally, you used transitions to prevent the reader from becoming confused as he or she reviews your writing.
Written Expression: Style	The student response establishes and maintains an effective style, while attending to the norms and conventions of the discipline. The response uses precise language consistently, including descriptive words and phrases, sensory details, linking and transitional words, words to indicate tone, and/or domain-specific vocabulary.	It is clear that you wrote the essay and were able to maintain the strong start by having a strong finish. Your writing was interesting because you used a variety of techniques you learned in your English class like using similes, metaphors, and sensory details.
Writing: Knowledge of Language and Conventions	The student response demonstrates command of the conventions of standard English consistent with effectively edited writing. Though there may be a few minor errors in grammar and usage, meaning is clear throughout the response.	You may have made a couple of mistakes, but these errors do not detract from the points you are trying to make. You may also have had a moment to proofread for common mistakes such as misspellings and problems with subject-verb agreement.

Now that you know how you will be assessed, you need a plan to get the most points possible on this essay. Here are the steps that you are going to take to create your essay for the Research Simulation Task:

1. Determine what points were important by reviewing your notes.
2. Write the thesis statement and the restatement.
3. Write your body paragraphs, citing evidence as you go.
4. Write your introduction and conclusion.
5. Revise and edit as necessary.

This might seem a little out of order. Your teacher might tell you, "Begin with the introduction, then develop it, then write a body paragraph, et cetera, et cetera, et cetera." That is good instruction and perfect for the classroom. It is not so good when you have only 85 minutes to read, review, answer multiple-choice questions, and write an essay.

This is a timed test. The goal is for you to get the best score that you possibly can in the time allotted. One of the main things that the readers want to see is an organized essay; a major part of having your essay clearly written is to have the thesis and restatement. Writing these two pieces of the essay first creates bookends for you. Because you are composing an essay on the computer, the restatement of the thesis will move down the page as you write, helping you to maintain your focus as you create the body paragraphs.

Remember, the thesis is what your essay is about. The body of the essay proves or demonstrates the point you made in your thesis and the restatement ensures that those points have been made.

The danger in spending too much time crafting a catchy introduction and then developing your essay is that you might simply run out of time. If you follow the steps outlined above, you at least have a structured essay if you only get to complete step three.

You are not expected to write a five-paragraph essay. If you can make your point in three, four, or six paragraphs, you will not be penalized. Sometimes essays that are shorter receive more points than those that are longer because brief essays have less fluff. If you find yourself writing, "It seems to me in my own opinion that this problem was not solved" or "In my opinion, I feel that…," you are putting filler in your essay. Don't fluff and stuff.

That being said, please reserve the three-paragraph essay for when you are running low on time. Having a short, concise essay that is relatively error-free will garner you more points than an unfinished essay (an introductory paragraph and one body paragraph), an outline, or no essay at all.

Writing Your Thesis

Review your evidence. Once you determine what points the authors have made, you should be able to craft your thesis statement. Remember, you can restate the question to create your thesis statement.

Here is a reprint of the directions for the analysis of the argument:

Directions: You have read an excerpt from a book and an article and watched a video describing "Shoeless" Joe Jackson and the 1919 World Series scandal. All three sources contain information that supports the claim that Jackson was an honest player. Carefully consider the argument each author uses to demonstrate Jackson's lack of involvement in the scandal. Write an essay that analyzes the strength of the arguments related to Jackson's innocence in at least two of the three supporting materials. Remember to use textual evidence to support your ideas.

We underlined what the question is asking you to do; it is asking you to identify the strongest argument. You're going to put that in your thesis statement with your opinion of what the strongest argument is. You will spend the body of the essay writing about it.

Your thesis statement might read:

Although there are many arguments the authors made about "Shoeless" Joe's innocence in an attempt to have him play baseball again, the most convincing argument is that _____.

The restatement of the thesis does not mean that you copy and paste the thesis statement again. That's bush league (pun intended). The goal of the restatement is to have the same ideas but presented in another way. Try it:

Of the many arguments presented to get baseball's ban lifted from Joe Jackson, the most convincing is clearly _____.

As you write one, you can revise and edit the other. Make whichever sentence you feel is the stronger of the two the thesis statement and the other the restatement.

If you cannot develop your restatement immediately, it might mean that your thesis statement is not that great. Look back at the question for help.

Let's try this with the directions that ask us to explain baseball's impact on American culture. Here's the reprint:

Directions: You have read an excerpt from a book and an article, watched a video describing "Shoeless" Joe Jackson and the 1919 World Series scandal, and examined a painting of a baseball game. All four sources contain depictions of baseball as a part of American culture. Carefully consider how baseball influences Americans. Using at least three of the four sources, write an essay that explains how baseball is part of American culture. Remember to use textual evidence to support your ideas.

Again, we have underlined the part of the prompt that indicates specifically what you are to do. For this essay, you might want to explain two specific things in detail. Even though you are asked to cite three of the four sources, you are looking for ideas expressed across the sources. You won't be analyzing one source at a time.

The thesis statement below would be perfect for a four-paragraph essay that would suit this purpose.

> Throughout the twentieth century, baseball played an integral part in American culture as evidenced by _____ and _____.

Again, as soon as you have the thesis, write it again in another way.

> After examining the sources, it is clear to see that baseball has played a role in American culture in the twentieth century because it _____ and _____.

These thesis statements are NO-NOs:

- **Fluff and stuff:** In my personal opinion, it seems to me that baseball, I think anyway, is pretty important to Americans.
- **Prove what you already know:** Shoeless Joe Jackson was a baseball player.
- **Announcements:** In today's essay, I'm going to write about what baseball meant to American culture.
- **Nonsensical thesis:** There is baseball in American culture for Americans which is important to them.

The Body Paragraphs

Remember that as you respond to the essay question, you are to synthesize the information in the texts instead of addressing one text at a time. Your body paragraphs should have evidence cited from more than one source to make your point.

Ideally, the outline of the essay should look like:

- Introduction with thesis
- Point One with evidence from two texts
- Point Two with evidence from two texts
- Point Three with evidence from two texts (if time permits)
- Conclusion with restatement of thesis.

It should NOT look like

- Introduction with thesis
- Analysis of text one
- Analysis of text two
- Analysis of text three
- Conclusion with restatement

If you follow the suggested method of organizing the body paragraphs, then it will be easier to create transitions from one idea to the next. Observe the difference between the following two examples:

Sample One

After this had happened, it was evident that the game of baseball would never be the same again.

Despite this setback, Americans relied upon the game to entertain them during the darkest days of the Great Depression. Two of the authors explain that Americans were eager to forget their troubles.

Sample Two

The author makes this point very clearly. He believed that baseball would never be the same again.

The second author partially agrees with the first author, but he makes another point. He makes the point that Americans needed entertainment during the Great Depression .

The second sample relies upon an analysis of the authors and the individual arguments that they make. That's not what the PARCC wants you to do; you are supposed to review all of the information presented to you and make a coherent analysis of all of it. This is a skill that you will use your entire life. If you consider the kinds of conversations you have with your friends and family, you naturally would discuss issues in the way exemplified in the first sample; that is, you would make a point and then support your point with different sources.

The Introduction and Conclusion

After you have written your body paragraphs, go back to write the introduction. Remember, the introduction prepares the reader for the rest of the essay, so begin with something catchy. An easy way to do this is to start with a quotation or a statistic; if you can't think of one, it's okay to use one from one of the sources.

Another way to get your reader interested in your essay is to tell a brief story, called an anecdote. If you have anything personal to add to the essay, this would be a good time to do it.

Aside from restating the thesis, the concluding paragraph sums up the ideas presented in the body paragraphs. For each body paragraph you have, write a sentence that summarizes that paragraph in the conclusion. After the ideas are wrapped up, authors generally end with a final thought. Do not use the conclusion to introduce a new idea. The place to introduce a new idea is in the body.

Here's an example of an introduction using an anecdote and a conclusion with a final thought. The thesis statement and restatements are underlined:

When I was young, I played tee ball. I didn't play very well, but luckily, neither did anyone else. My teammate, Karla, hit the ball off the tee, then ran to what she thought was first base. It was third. I cheered for her anyway; in fact, our whole team cheered for her. When she reached the base, the umpire declared her safe, then escorted her to first base. While I know now that running to third base instead of first is not legal in baseball, when I was six, her violation of the rule did not prevent me from enjoying myself and that game. Everyone, even the parents, enjoyed themselves. It seems that people can look past a mistake of one person and still enjoy a baseball game. <u>The authors of the texts and the video demonstrate that baseball remains an enjoyable pastime despite some problems.</u>

Body Paragraph One discusses a major problem and reinforces the idea that people enjoy the game anyway.

Body Paragraph Two discusses a different problem and continues the discussion that people enjoy the game.

<u>Through the years, baseball has had many violations of the rules, but these problems have not stopped people from enjoying the game.</u> It seems that people are more willing to look for the positive aspects of the game than worry about upon the negative points. Discuss Problem One and how people overlook it here; then discuss Problem Two and how people overlook it. For every one "bad" player on the team, there are another eight men on the field who are playing an honest game. Their efforts should not be forgotten because of one person's misdeed.

Working Through an RST

Let's work through an example together. We'll include the questions that would accompany the texts, but we will leave the answer choices out so they are not a distraction. At the end, we will provide a sample student essay.

Don't forget about the directions! Here they are. We will reprint them as we move through the exercise. Remember to ask and answer questions on the directions first.

Directions: Vincent Van Gogh is one of the most recognizable names in the art world today. However, Van Gogh did not enjoy success as an artist during his lifetime. Today, you will read three texts and view two of Van Gogh's self portraits to learn about Van Gogh's life. After you read, you will write an essay that explains how the events and relationships with his family shaped Van Gogh's view on the world.

What is the topic?	Vincent Van Gogh's family and events playing a role in his outlook on life
What sources will you use?	Three texts and two self-portraits
What type of essay will you write?	An explanation of how family and events shaped Van Gogh's perspective
What evidence will you need?	I'll definitely need information about his relationships with his family members. The directions mention events in his life, too.

Text	Questions

Text

Greenberg, Jan, and Sandra Jordan. *Vincent Van Gogh: Portrait of an Artist.* New York: Random House, 2001. (2001) From Chapter 1: "A Brabant Boy 1853–75"

I have nature and art and poetry, if that is not enough what is? — Letter to Theo, January 1874

On March 30, 1853, the handsome, soberly dressed Reverend Theodorus van Gogh entered the ancient town hall of Groot-Zundert, in the Brabant, a province of the Netherlands. He opened the birth register to number twenty-nine, where exactly one year earlier he had sadly written "Vincent Willem van Gogh, stillborn." Beside the inscription he wrote again "Vincent Willem van Gogh," the name of his new, healthy son, who was sleeping soundly next to his mother in the tiny parsonage across the square. The baby's arrival was an answered prayer for the still-grieving family.

The first Vincent lay buried in a tiny grave by the door of the church where Pastor van Gogh preached. The Vincent who lived grew to be a sturdy redheaded boy. Every Sunday on his way to church, young Vincent would pass the headstone carved with the name he shared. Did he feel as if his dead brother where the rightful Vincent, the one who would remain perfect in his parents' hearts, and that he was merely an unsatisfactory replacement? That might have been one of the reasons he spent so much of his life feeling like a lonely outsider, as if he didn't fit anywhere in the world.

Despite his dramatic beginning, Vincent had an ordinary childhood, giving no hint of the painter he would become. The small parsonage, with an upstairs just two windows wide under a slanting roof, quickly grew crowded. By the time he was six he had two sisters, Anna and Elizabeth, and one brother, Theo, whose gentle nature made him their mother's favorite.

Media Text
The Van Gogh Gallery, a commercial Web resource with links to Van Gogh's art and information about his life:
http://www.vangoghgallery.com/

Questions

Question One

Part A
What is the purpose of including the quotation from Van Gogh's letter to his brother Theo?

Part B
The author implies that there is a difference between Theo's personality and Van Gogh's. What is it?

Question Two

Part A
What references to religion are made in the text?

Part B
What effect does the religious references have upon the text?

Question Three

Part A
What does the author imply about the Van Gogh family?

Part B
What evidence from the text supports your response to Part A?

Text	Questions
From: "The Troubled Life of Vincent Van Gogh" by Bonnie Butterfield http://bonniebutterfield.com/VincentVanGogh.htm Most casual art lovers see Van Gogh as a troubled, but successful artist in the eyes of society. This is true today, but he was not able to experience success during his life. Instead, he was taunted by children and run out of villages by people who feared his erratic and non-conforming behavior. He experienced failure in every occupational pursuit he attempted, including painting, and was marked by intermittent episodes of depression, violence and acting out behaviors. Thanks to the preservation of 1000's of letters Van Gogh had written to friends and family, especially to his brother Theo, we have a nearly complete understanding of his feelings, experiences, and views on every aspect of his life. Surprisingly, his incredible artistic talent went undeveloped and unrecognized until he was 27 years old, after he had already failed at two other career choices, as an art dealer and a Protestant minister. Under the shroud of family shame when he was found incompetent to follow in his father's ministerial foot steps, he began to study art. He obsessively poured himself into this newly found talent and completed thousands of sketches and oil paintings before he shot himself to death at the age of 37 years old. Many observers of Van Gogh's life justifiably believe that his eccentricities, which were visible from early childhood, compounded to create many distressing experiences that directly impacted his style of painting. The rudiments of Expressionism was born of these experiences. Therefore, a look into his childhood and life is imperative to understanding the development of his artistic style and the origins of Expressionism. Vincent's sister, Elizabeth Van Gogh, described his demeanor as a child. He was "intensely serious and uncommunicative, and walked around clumsily and in a daze, with his head hung low." She continued by saying, "Not only were his little sisters and brothers (he was the oldest of 8) like strangers to him, but he was a stranger to himself." A servant who worked for the Van Gogh family when Vincent was a child described him as an, "odd, aloof child who had queer manners and seemed more like an old man," than the child he was. Vincent was a disappointment to his mother, and eventually to his entire family, even his beloved brother Theo Van Gogh who supported him financially for the 10 years that he worked as a painter.	**Question Four** **Part A** The author writes, "Most casual art lovers see Van Gogh as a troubled, but successful artist in the eyes of society." How does the author contradict this statement in the introduction? **Part B** Where else in the text does the author use the same strategy? **Question Five** **Part A** The author makes a claim that one cannot understand Van Gogh's artwork without having an understanding of his childhood. How does she support this claim? **Part B** What evidence from the text provides a specific example of the author's claim from Part A? **Question Six** **Part A** How does the quote from Van Gogh's sister contribute to the author's thesis? **Part B** The author of the first text included this quote from Vincent to Theo, "I have nature and art and poetry, if that is not enough what is?" After reading the second text, what can be inferred about the relationship that Vincent had with his brother?

Text	Questions
"Revealing The Many Faces of Vincent Van Gogh On His 161st Birthday" The Huffington Post | by Katherine Brooks Posted: 03/30/2014 10:06 am EDT Updated: 03/30/2014 10:59 am EDT Today marks the birthday of Vincent van Gogh, the Dutch post-Impressionist who brought the world unforgettable visions of sunflowers and starry nights. Born on this day 161 years ago, the painter ranks among the most recognizable (not to mention expensive) artists to have ever existed, filling the halls of major museums from the Louvre to the Met to the Rijksmuseum. Most contemporary accounts of the venerable artist present a van Gogh unappreciated in his own time. Painting throughout the late 19th century, he died—of self-inflicted wounds—before he ever reached the status of a "successful" painter, leaving behind a trove of unsold paintings that wound their way to the possession of van Gogh's sister-in-law, Johanna van Gogh-Bonger. She's part of the reason his name ever reached the ears and lips of major gallerists and curators, as she spearheaded the efforts behind the influential 1905 exhibition staged at the Stedelijk Museum in Amsterdam. History speculates with intense curiosity on what van Gogh was like during his life, at times alleging he cut his ear off in a fit of unrequited love (a story heavily contested by some scholars) and other times surmising the great artistic talent suffered from color blindness. With a century and a half to wonder who the man beneath the straw hat is, and pore over his personal letters, we've really only uncovered a caricature of what Vincent was probably like. This much we know—he was self—taught, enraptured by the innovation of neo-Impressionists, supported and pushed to creative limits by his brother and eventually alienated by his own mental turmoil. In honor of yet another anniversary of Vincent van Gogh's birth, we let our own curiosity run wild while perusing the many self-portraits the tortured artist produced. From dark color palettes rendered in chaotic brushstrokes to luminescent imaginings captured in his signature saturated hues, the collection of faces reveal—at the very least—how the painter viewed himself. Scroll through the selection below and let us know how you're celebrating the art holiday in the comments.	**Question Seven** **Part A** The author explains that Van Gogh was responsible for bringing the world "unforgettable visions of sunflowers and starry nights." How are these images contrasted in the body of the text? **Part B** What evidence from the text supports your response to Part A? **Question Eight** **Part A** The author mentions that there is a lot of curiosity about Vincent Van Gogh's life. In what ways does she lead the reader to believe that there is more to Van Gogh than what scholars have learned through his letters? **Part B** Of the evidence presented, which three of the following claims suggest that Vincent Van Gogh overcame challenges in his own lifetime? **Question Nine** **Part A** In what way is Van Gogh's family portrayed in this article? **Part B** How is this portrayal different from what was portrayed in the other texts?

Text	Questions
These photographs of Van Gogh's self-portraits are courtesy of SuperStock.  	**Question Ten** **Part A** There are many differences in the techniques used to create the two self-portraits such as the use of brushstrokes, the source of light, and the use of line. One readily noticeable difference is the use of color. How does Van Gogh depict different emotions through the use of color? **Part B** In the article from the Huffington Post, the author writes, "With a century and a half to wonder who the man beneath the straw hat is, and pore over his personal letters, we've really only uncovered a caricature of what Vincent was probably like." In the portraits provided, one has a straw hat; the other does not. What might the authors of the three articles surmise is the reason that the straw hat is removed in the later portrait?

Essay Question

Directions: You have read an excerpt from a text, a blog entry, and an online article and viewed two of Van Gogh's self-portraits. All four sources support the claim that Van Gogh experienced problems in his life that contributed to his outlook on the world. Carefully consider how Van Gogh interacted with the world around him. Using at least three of the four sources, write an essay that explains how these relationships and events shaped Van Gogh's perspective on the world. Remember to use textual evidence to support your ideas. You may cite the textual evidence by using Source A, Source B, Source C, and Source D.

The sources are:

Source A: *Vincent Van Gogh: Portrait of an Artist* by Jan Greenberg and Sandra Jordan

Source B: "The Troubled Life of Vincent Van Gogh" by Bonnie Butterfield
http://bonniebutterfield.com/VincentVanGogh.htm

Source C: "Revealing the Many Faces of Vincent Van Gogh on His 161st Birthday" by Katherine Brooks
The Huffington Post
http://www.huffingtonpost.com/2014/03/30/vincent-van-gogh_n_5051910.html

Source D: SuperStock: (Image 1) Stock Photo: Self Portrait 1888 Vincent van Gogh (1853–1890/Dutch) https://www.superstock.com/stock-photography/900-428#id=3999. (Image 2) Self-Portrait in Front of Easel 1888, Vincent van Gogh (1853–1890/ Dutch) Oil on Canvas Van Gogh Museum, Amsterdam. https://www.superstock.com/stock-photography/900-101467#id=23169

Portion of the Essay	Student Essay	Analysis
Introduction	A lot of people use the term "struggling artist" to describe a career in art. What defines success for artists? Is it recognition? Is it money? It seems that paintings are valuable only if they make it to a gallery or a museum, and with so much art in the world, the competition is tough, which may make artists feel as if they struggle their entire lives. This was certainly the case for Vincent Van Gogh. From his birth to his death, the relationships that Van Gogh had with his family and failures he experienced in his career affected his view of the world and because of that, much of the artwork Van Gogh produced reflected his troubled soul.	The student begins with a term that he has probably heard before, maybe in art class, to describe artists. He then writes a rhetorical question and provides suggestions for the answer to this question by posing two more rhetorical questions. After suggesting that recognition or money defines success for artists, the student asserts that a way to be successful as an artist is to have one's work shown. He then adds that this is a challenge, and because getting gallery space is so challenging, artists don't feel successful. This leads him to focus his attention upon Van Gogh. The student then writes the thesis statement; it lays out the rest of the essay for us. We should see a discussion of his family, then one about his career.
Body Paragraph One	Van Gogh experienced many problems in his relationship with his immediate family. His sister is quoted as saying, "Not only were his little sisters and brothers like strangers to him, but he was a stranger to himself" (Source B). The authors of Source A speculate that a reason for this estrangement might be that Van Gogh felt that he did not fit in with the family because he shared a name with a baby who was stillborn and that he was a poor imitation of the baby who did not live. Because his father was a minister, the family lived near the church and Van Gogh probably saw this reminder on a daily basis.	The student asserts that Van Gogh felt like a stranger in his own family and uses reasons from the first and second sources to support his reasoning. The student has probably used the information from questions 3 and 6 to assist him with this response.

Portion of the Essay	Student Essay	Analysis
Body Paragraph Two	Van Gogh shared his name with his dead, stillborn brother, but Van Gogh's younger brother, Theo, who is described as his mother's favorite, was named after his father (Source A). Even though Vincent may have viewed Theo as the favored brother, it seems that Theo did his best to support Vincent emotionally and financially. We know that Vincent and Theo corresponded for years, that Theo supported Vincent financially as Vincent painted, and that it is likely that Theo's wife is the person responsible for making Vincent's artwork popular (Sources B and C). Regardless of his use of "dark color palettes rendered in chaotic brushstrokes to luminescent imaginings captured in his signature saturated hues," which was a style that was new and daring for the time, his brother Theo supported Vincent's efforts as an artist (Source C).	The student continues the discussion of the family impact by focusing specifically on the relationship that Van Gogh had with his brothers. He has made the transition from one paragraph to the next by restating the information about sharing a name with a stillborn. The student then provides evidence of how Theo was viewed as a favorite and how Theo supported Vincent throughout his life. The student has cited evidence from three of the sources in this paragraph, meeting the requirement set out by the directions. Most likely, the student is using information from questions 1, 3, 6, and 8 to assist him in his response.

Portion of the Essay	Student Essay	Analysis
Body Paragraph Three	Even though Vincent received emotional and financial support to pursue his career in art, he was not a successful artist while he was alive. This was the third career in which Van Gogh failed, making him feel like a great disappointment to his family because he could not even be a preacher like his father was (Source B). His depression can be seen in the two self portraits. In the 1887 portrait, Van Gogh uses bright colors like bright yellow for the straw hat, light tan for his suit, a light blue shadow on his head and clothes, and a hint of blue sky implied with bright blue brush strokes. A year later, the background is a darker, solid blue, his clothes are brown instead of tan, and his happy yellow straw hat is gone.	The student makes the transition from the discussion about his brother to Van Gogh's career choices by mentioning again how Theo supported Vincent. He supports this claim with evidence from Source B. Part of the thesis statement is that Van Gogh's artwork "reflected a troubled soul," so the student provides a quick analysis of the two paintings from Source D. This is evidence using Question Ten, Parts A and B in his response.
Conclusion	Through this quick analysis of his self portraits, it is clear to see that Van Gogh experienced problems throughout his life. Vincent Van Gogh expressed his pain through his art, not knowing that he perceived was an image created by a "failure" would have a great impact on the art world.	The student makes a transition from the analysis of the self-portraits to the restatement of the thesis. He concludes the essay with a final thought; that Van Gogh perceived he was a failure when the art world considers Van Gogh a success.

Commentary

This essay would earn a 4, or full credit, on the PARCC's draft rubric. It demonstrates that the student has a clear understanding of all of the texts and that he was able to incorporate more than one into his response. The author does an excellent job synthesizing information from two or more sources, best exemplified in body paragraph two. The logic that the author uses is based in the evidence that goes across the texts; for example, the author draws a conclusion about his parents' choices in names for Vincent and Theo from more than one text. The essay is well-organized: there is a clear introductory paragraph with a thesis, supporting evidence, transitions between paragraphs, and a concluding paragraph with a restatement of the thesis. The author maintains a formal style to appropriately address the readers and it is evident that he had time to proofread his response as there are no grammatical errors.

CHAPTER REVIEW

> Read the directions carefully. They provide you with guidance for collecting evidence.

> Part of the evidence is the source of the text. Consider when the text was written and what website published it.

> When you read the essay prompt, pay special attention to exactly what the question is asking of you. If your response does not answer the question adequately, you will not get credit, regardless of how good your essay might be.

> As you write your essay, strengthen your essay by citing the evidence from the text to provide specific examples.

Practice Test— Performance-Based Assessment

Practice the PARCC Performance-Based Assessment

Now it is time to try a PBA on your own. Time yourself as you take the assessment. The answer key and sample essays are at the end of each section of the PBA.

Part One

Research Simulation Task

85 minutes

Directions: A diner is a restaurant that is undeniably American. Today, you will read two nonfiction selections about diners and view a painting of a diner to learn about the diner's place in American culture. When you are finished reading, you will write an essay that synthesizes the information that you have learned about the American diner.

The first selection is an excerpt from *Travels with Charley: In Search of America* by John Steinbeck. This selection was obtained from the Common Core State Standards Appendix B. In this nonfiction novel, Steinbeck travels across the country with his dog, Charley. While in New England, Steinbeck stops at a roadside diner.

Please read the excerpt and answer the questions that accompany it.

Steinbeck, John. *Travels with Charley: In Search of America*. New York: Penguin, 1997. (1962) From pages 27–28.

Travels with Charley: In Search of America

John Steinbeck

I soon discovered that if a wayfaring stranger wishes to eavesdrop on a local population the places for him to slip in and hold his peace are bars and churches. But some New England towns don't have bars, and church is only on Sunday. A good alternative is the roadside restaurant where men gather for breakfast before going to work or going hunting. To find these places inhabited one must get up very early. And there is a drawback even to this. Early-rising men not only do not talk much to strangers, they barely talk to one another. Breakfast conversation is limited to a series of laconic grunts. The natural New England taciturnity reaches its glorious perfection at breakfast.

I am not normally a breakfast eater, but here I had to be or I wouldn't see anybody unless I stopped for gas. At the first lighted roadside restaurant I pulled in and took my seat at a counter. The customers were folded over their coffee cups like ferns. A normal conversation is as follows:

WAITRESS: "Same?"

CUSTOMER: "Yep."

WAITRESS: "Cold enough for you?"

CUSTOMER: "Yep."

(Ten minutes.)

WAITRESS: "Refill?"

CUSTOMER: "Yep."

This is a really talkative customer.

Question One

Part A
Which of the choices below best express Steinbeck's purpose in visiting the diner in New England?

- ○ A. He wanted to eat breakfast.
- ○ B. He wanted to visit a typical New England town because he was thinking of moving there.
- ○ C. He wanted evidence so that he could portray a characteristic of the New England population.
- ○ D. He wanted to find out how the hunters were doing this season.

Part B

In the boxes below, please choose three details from the excerpt that support your selection for Part A.

1. "I soon discovered that if a wayfaring stranger wishes to eavesdrop on a local population the places for him to slip in and hold his peace are bars and churches."

2. "A good alternative is the roadside restaurant where men gather for breakfast before going to work or going hunting."

3. "To find these places inhabited one must get up very early."

4. "Early-rising men not only do not talk much to strangers, they barely talk to one another."

5. "The natural New England taciturnity reaches its glorious perfection at breakfast."

6. "At the first lighted roadside restaurant I pulled in and took my seat at a counter."

7. "The customers were folded over their coffee cups like ferns."

Response One
Response Two
Response Three

Question Two

Part A

As used in Steinbeck's excerpt, the word *taciturnity* most closely means...

○ **A.** chatty   ○ **C.** quiet
○ **B.** spiritual   ○ **D.** grumpy

Part B

What evidence from the text best supports your response?

○ **A.** "Early-rising men not only do not talk much to strangers, they barely talk to one another."
○ **B.** "A good alternative is the roadside restaurant where men gather for breakfast before going to work or going hunting."
○ **C.** "This is a really talkative customer."
○ **D.** "But some New England towns don't have bars, and church is only on Sunday."

Question Three

Part A

What irony exists in Steinbeck's position as a "wayfaring stranger"?

○ **A.** As a "wayfaring stranger," Steinbeck has to get people to like him before they like his dog, Charley.
○ **B.** As a "wayfaring stranger," Steinbeck has to "hold his peace" to get any information on what is going on in the town.
○ **C.** As a "wayfaring stranger," Steinbeck needs to establish a relationship with the waitress so that the men in the diner will respect him.
○ **D.** As a "wayfaring stranger," Steinbeck is encouraged to leave town.

Part B

Which best explanation best supports your response to Part A?

○ **A.** Steinbeck is trying to get information on the town. His usual way of doing this is to go to a church or a bar, but because he cannot go to either one of these establishments, he goes to a roadside restaurant.
○ **B.** Steinbeck wants to talk to the men so that he can get information about the town from them. They won't do this until he can prove that he is friendly with the waitress.
○ **C.** Steinbeck describes the people of New England as quiet, but he has to be quiet in order to gather information about them.
○ **D.** As a famous writer, John Steinbeck is usually welcomed everywhere he goes, but because the people in this town are so grumpy, they encourage him to leave town.

Question Four

Part A

Steinbeck characterizes breakfast chatter as "glorious perfection" of a New England characteristic. How does he illustrate this in the excerpt?

- ○ A. Steinbeck provides a sample of dialogue between a waitress and a customer.
- ○ B. Steinbeck contrasts conversations from the church with conversations at the diner.
- ○ C. Steinbeck describes what he eats at the diner and the other patrons' reaction to his choice of breakfast.
- ○ D. Steinbeck provides a description of a typical encounter at a gas station is like, what a conversation at church is like, what he overheard at a bar, and what was said at a diner.

Part B

Which of the following choices best summarizes Steinbeck's feelings about the characteristic he observed?

- ○ A. "I soon discovered that if a wayfaring stranger wishes to eavesdrop on a local population the places for him to slip in and hold his peace are bars and churches."
- ○ B. "And there is a drawback even to this."
- ○ C. "I am not normally a breakfast eater, but here I had to be or I wouldn't see anybody unless I stopped for gas."
- ○ D. "This is a really talkative customer."

The second nonfiction piece is from an article from the American Diner Museum entitled, "Diner History and Culture." It was obtained from their website at *http://www.americandinermuseum.org/site/history.php*. Please read the article and answer the questions that accompany it.

Diner History and Culture

What is a diner?

A true "diner" is a prefabricated structure built at an assembly site and transported to a permanent location for installation to serve prepared food. Webster's Dictionary defines a diner as "a restaurant in the shape of a railroad car." The word "diner" is a derivative of "dining car" and diner designs reflected the styling that manufacturers borrowed from railroad dining cars. A diner is usually outfitted with a counter, stools and a food preparation or service area along the back wall. Decommissioned railroad passenger cars and trolleys were often converted into diners by those who could not afford to purchase a new diner.

How diners began

The origins of the diner can be traced to Walter Scott, a part-time pressman and type compositor in Providence, Rhode Island. Around 1858 when Scott was 17 years old he supplemented his income by selling sandwiches and coffee from a basket to newspaper night workers and patrons of men's club rooms. By 1872 business became so lucrative that Scott quit his printing work and began to sell food at night from a horse-drawn covered express wagon parked outside the Providence Journal newspaper office. In doing so, Walter Scott unknowingly inspired the birth of what would become one of America's most recognized icons—the diner.

Over the decades

The success of the early converted wagons inspired a few individuals to form companies and manufacture lunch wagons for sale. These improved wagons allowed customers to stand inside, protected from inclement weather or sit on stools at counters. Night lunch wagons or "Nite Owls" began to appear in many New England towns and cities during the late 1800's. Some models were elaborate and were fitted with stained and etched glass windows, intricately painted murals and fancy woodwork. The lunch wagons became very popular because workers and pedestrians could purchase inexpensive meals during the day but especially at night when most restaurants closed by 8:00 pm.

Because of the attraction to the lucrative trade, lunch wagon vendors became so abundant on the streets that many towns and cities passed ordinances to restrict hours of operation. This prompted some owners to circumvent the law by positioning their wagons on semi-permanent locations. At the same time that lunch wagons were becoming popular, obsolete horse drawn streetcars were being replaced by electrified models. Many of the displaced cars were purchased and converted into food venues for a fraction of the cost of a new dining car. Operating on meager budgets, most owners were more concerned with making a living than maintaining their car. Dining cars took on the reputation of the "greasy spoon" and gathering places for the unsavory elements of the community.

Question Five

Part A

In the conclusion, the authors state, "Dining cars took on the reputation of the 'greasy spoon' and gathering places for the unsavory elements of the community." From the context of the sentence, what is a "greasy spoon"?

○ A. A spoon that has a lot of grease upon it and can't be washed easily.
○ B. A restaurant where criminals hang out.
○ C. A restaurant that is not clean and does not serve good food.
○ D. A restaurant that is only open at night.

Part B

How does the article contrast the description of the "greasy spoon"? Select two pieces of evidence from the text that demonstrate a different view of the diner.

1. "Some models were elaborate and were fitted with stained and etched glass windows, intricately painted murals and fancy woodwork."

2. "Around 1858 when Scott was 17 years old he supplemented his income by selling sandwiches and coffee from a basket to newspaper night workers and patrons of men's club rooms."

3. "The lunch wagons became very popular because workers and pedestrians could purchase inexpensive meals during the day but especially at night when most restaurants closed by 8:00 pm."

4. "Night lunch wagons or 'Nite Owls' began to appear in many New England towns and cities during the late 1800's."

5. "Many of the displaced cars were purchased and converted into food venues for a fraction of the cost of a new dining car."

Evidence One

Evidence Two

Question Six

Part A

The authors claim that the diner is "an icon." What is an icon?

○ A. A figment of someone's imagination.
○ B. A lunch wagon.
○ C. A representative symbol.
○ D. A gathering place for a community.

Part B

In which way(s) do the authors support this claim? Select three statements from the article that provide support that "diners are icons," and drag and drop them to the boxes below.

1	"Some models were elaborate and were fitted with stained and etched glass windows, intricately painted murals and fancy woodwork."
2	"Decommissioned railroad passenger cars and trolleys were often converted into diners by those who could not afford to purchase a new diner."
3	"Because of the attraction to the lucrative trade, lunch wagon vendors became so abundant on the streets that many towns and cities passed ordinances to restrict hours of operation."
4	"The success of the early converted wagons inspired a few individuals to form companies and manufacture lunch wagons for sale."
5	"Dining cars took on the reputation of the 'greasy spoon' and gathering places for the unsavory elements of the community."
6	"A true 'diner' is a prefabricated structure built at an assembly site and transported to a permanent location for installation to serve prepared food."
7	"The origins of the diner can be traced to Walter Scott, a part-time pressman and type compositor in Providence, Rhode Island."
8	"The word 'diner' is a derivative of 'dining car' and diner designs reflected the styling that manufacturers borrowed from railroad dining cars."
9	"Because of the attraction to the lucrative trade, lunch wagon vendors became so abundant on the streets that many towns and cities passed ordinances to restrict hours of operation."

Evidence One
Evidence Two
Evidence Three

Question Seven

Part A

The purpose of the article is to

- ○ A. educate people about the quality of diner food.
- ○ B. explain the history of the diner.
- ○ C. supplement Steinbeck's explanation of diner service.
- ○ D. defend diner owners from criticism about restaurant ownership.

Part B

Which of the following statements best supports your choice for Part A?

- ○ A. The introduction of the article provides a definition from a dictionary. Later in the article, there is an explanation of the different types of diners and how they came to be, attributing the creation to one man in Providence.
- ○ B. Steinbeck felt that no one would understand his sense of humor as he tried to explain what the conversation was like at the diner he was at. He contacted the American Diner Museum and asked them to write an article to assist his readers.
- ○ C. The article states that diner owners were "more concerned with making a living than maintaining their car." Clearly, as the restaurant itself fell apart, the quality of the food went down.
- ○ D. Diner food has never been of good quality. This is why diner owners were able to open early, stay open later than other restaurants, and provide cheap meals to people who only had a moment to grab lunch.

Question Eight

Both Steinbeck and The American Diner Museum discuss diners. Read the statements listed below. Then, drag and drop the statements in the boxes in which Steinbeck, the American Diner Museum, or both would agree. Not all statements will be used.

Statements about Diners

1	Diners make good meeting places because they are open every day.
2	Diners became popular because they provided inexpensive meals during the lunch rush.
3	You can find diners in New England.
4	Diners are for locals.
5	Most diner owners are not concerned with food quality.
6	You can get to know the population of a town by going to a diner in the morning.
7	No other type of restaurant offers as many choices as a diner does.
8	Diners are open longer hours than regular restaurants.
9	The wait staff generally provides friendly service.

Steinbeck	American Diner Museum	Both

Nighthawks by Edward Hopper, 1942. Oil on canvas.
Courtesy of The Art Institute of Chicago.

Question Nine

From the following statements, select five from the two texts that would describe this painting. Drag and drop the statement into the response boxes below.

Author	Statement
Steinbeck	1. "A good alternative is the roadside restaurant where men gather for breakfast before going to work or going hunting."
Steinbeck	2. "To find these places inhabited one must get up very early."
Steinbeck	3. "At the first lighted roadside restaurant I pulled in and took my seat at a counter."
Steinbeck	4. "The customers were folded over their coffee cups like ferns."
American Diner Museum	5. "A diner is usually outfitted with a counter, stools and a food preparation or service area along the back wall."
American Diner Museum	6. "Around 1858 when Scott was 17 years old he supplemented his income by selling sandwiches and coffee from a basket to newspaper night workers and patrons of men's club rooms."
American Diner Museum	7. "Night lunch wagons or 'Nite Owls' began to appear in many New England towns and cities during the late 1800's."
American Diner Museum	8. "The lunch wagons became very popular because workers and pedestrians could purchase inexpensive meals during the day but especially at night when most restaurants closed by 8:00 pm."

Responses

Description One
Description Two
Description Three
Description Four
Description Five

Question Ten

Part A

Which of the following best describe the significance of the title of this painting?

- ○ A. The people portrayed are working late at night.
- ○ B. The street is cold and empty, but the people inside the diner are happy and warm.
- ○ C. The customers might be at the diner because they are scheming.
- ○ D. Just out of view of the painting, a large bird of prey sits upon the cigar sign.

Part B

Which of the following statements best supports your response for Part A?

- ○ A. The men must have just finished their jobs late at night because they are both in their suits. The man behind the counter is clearly working. The woman is a wife or girlfriend of the man with whom she sits.
- ○ B. The street is painted in dark brown and black; it looks dark and cold. In contrast, the scene inside the diner is painted yellow, which is a warm color. Because the people have coffee, they are warm, which makes them happy.
- ○ C. The customers are sitting in a way in which they can see and talk to each other. If they did not want to talk, they would be sitting in a row, facing the back wall. They are meeting at a diner when the streets are clear and no one else, save the man working the counter, will see or hear them. They are not eating; each has a cup of coffee, maybe to keep awake.
- ○ D. The sign above the diner that advertises cigars has a bird perched upon it; its talon can be seen after the "s" in "Phillies". That bird is a lookout for the people who are in the diner. It protects them from people who may want to hurt them.

Essay Question

Directions: The two texts and the painting each relate information about American diners. As you see it, what is the role of the American diner? Please support your response with examples from the three sources. You may cite them as Source A, Source B, and Source C or by the authors' names.

Source A: excerpt from John Steinbeck's *Travels with Charley: In Search of America*.

Source B: *Diner History and Culture* from The American Diner Museum

Source C: *Nighthawks* by Edward Hopper (1942 oil on canvas)

PREWRITING SPACE
Use the space provided to make a writing plan for your essay.

Begin your essay here

Part Two

Literary Analysis

80 Minutes

Directions: Today you will analyze a poem and a passage from a text. As you read these texts, you will gather information and answer questions about the authors' use of language to describe the city of Chicago so you can write an analytical essay.

Sandburg, Carl. "Chicago." *Chicago Poems.* New York: Henry Holt, 1916. (1916)

Chicago

Carl Sandburg

Hog Butcher for the World,

Tool Maker, Stacker of Wheat,

Player with Railroads and the Nation's Freight Handler;

Stormy, husky, brawling,

City of the Big Shoulders:

They tell me you are wicked and I believe them, for I

    have seen your painted women under the gas lamps

    luring the farm boys.

And they tell me you are crooked and I answer: Yes, it

    is true I have seen the gunman kill and go free to

    kill again.

And they tell me you are brutal and my reply is: On the

    faces of women and children I have seen the marks

    of wanton hunger.

And having answered so I turn once more to those who

    sneer at this my city, and I give them back the sneer

    and say to them:

Come and show me another city with lifted head singing

    so proud to be alive and coarse and strong and cunning.

Flinging magnetic curses amid the toil of piling job on

    job, here is a tall bold slugger set vivid against the

    little soft cities;

Fierce as a dog with tongue lapping for action, cunning

    as a savage pitted against the wilderness,

Bareheaded,

Shoveling,

Wrecking,

Planning,

Building, breaking, rebuilding,

Under the smoke, dust all over his mouth, laughing with

    white teeth,

Under the terrible burden of destiny laughing as a young

    man laughs,

Laughing even as an ignorant fighter laughs who has

    never lost a battle,

Bragging and laughing that under his wrist is the pulse,

    and under his ribs the heart of the people,

        Laughing!

Laughing the stormy, husky, brawling laughter of

    Youth, half-naked, sweating, proud to be Hog

    Butcher, Tool Maker, Stacker of Wheat, Player with

    Railroads and Freight Handler to the Nation.

Question One

Part A

How does Sandburg begin this poem?

- ○ A. He provides a history of the city.
- ○ B. He asks the reader to follow him to Chicago.
- ○ C. He lists the names that the city has been called.
- ○ D. He describes what the city has been doing with the nation's resources.

Part B

How does the introduction play a crucial role in the development of this poem?
Select all that apply.

- ☐ A. He uses the introduction for an explanation of what the city is like.
- ☐ B. He shows how Chicago has moved from an industrial town to become spoiled by evils like hunger, disease, and crime.
- ☐ C. He repeats the names in the conclusion to place emphasis on the importance that the city of Chicago has.
- ☐ D. He uses the introduction as a foundation to create central image of the poem: a working man.

Question Two

Part A

Sandburg states that people have criticized the city. How does he answer the critics?

- ○ A. He explains that the city has experienced troubles like fire, disease, and crime, but that they are working on improving conditions.
- ○ B. He infers that the people who founded Chicago were selfish, but the people who have just moved to Chicago are adding cultural relevance to the city.
- ○ C. He asks the critics to find another city that has as many hard-working, fighting people like Chicago and implies that the industry defines the city.
- ○ D. He agrees with the critics and adds more criticism to the city.

Part B

What evidence from the poem supports your response to Part A? Select all that apply.

☐ A. "proud to be Hog
   Butcher, Tool Maker, Stacker of Wheat, Player with
   Railroads and Freight Handler to the Nation."

☐ B. "And they tell me you are brutal and my reply is: On the
   faces of women and children I have seen the marks
   of wanton hunger."

☐ C. "And they tell me you are crooked and I answer: Yes, it
   is true I have seen the gunman kill and go free to
   kill again. "

☐ D. "Come and show me another city with lifted head singing
   so proud to be alive and coarse and strong and cunning.
   Flinging magnetic curses amid the toil of piling job on
   job, here is a tall bold slugger set vivid against the
   little soft cities;"

Murphy, Jim. *The Great Fire.* New York: Scholastic, 1995. (1995)
From Chapter 1: "A City Ready to Burn."

A City Ready to Burn

Jim Murphy

Chicago in 1871 was a city ready to burn. The city boasted having 59,500 buildings, many of them—such as the Court-house and the Tribune Building—large and ornately decorated. The trouble was that about two-thirds of all these structures were made entirely of wood. Many of the remaining buildings (even the ones proclaimed to be "fireproof") looked solid, but were actually jerrybuilt affairs; the stone or brick exteriors hid wooden frames and floors, all topped with highly flammable tar or shingle roofs. It was also a common practice to disguise wood as another kind of building material. The fancy exterior decorations on just about every building were carved from wood, then painted to look like stone or marble. Most churches had steeples that appeared to be solid from the street, but a closer inspection would reveal a wooden framework covered with cleverly painted copper or tin.

The situation was worst in the middle-class and poorer districts. Lot sizes were small, and owners usually filled them up with cottages, barns, sheds, and outhouses—all made of fast-burning wood, naturally. Because both Patrick and Catherine O'Leary worked, they were able to put a large addition on their cottage despite a lot size of just 25 by 100 feet. Interspersed in these residential areas were a variety of businesses—paint factories, lumberyards, distilleries, gasworks, mills, furniture manufacturers, warehouses, and coal distributors.

Wealthier districts were by no means free of fire hazards. Stately stone and brick homes had wood interiors, and stood side by side with smaller wood-frame houses. Wooden stables and other storage buildings were common, and trees lined the streets and filled the yards.

Media Text The Great Chicago Fire, an exhibit created by the Chicago Historical Society that includes essays and images: *http://www.chicagohs.org/fire/intro/gcf-index.html*

Question Three

Part A
In the first paragraph, the author states that Chicago's buildings were "jerrybuilt affairs." What does that term mean?

○ A. The construction was crafted by a man named Jerry.
○ B. The construction was made entirely out of wood.
○ C. The construction looked solid, but it was not.
○ D. The construction was completed in one day.

Part B
What evidence from the text supports your response for Part A? Select all that apply.

☐ A. "… the stone or brick exteriors hid wooden frames and floors,…."
☐ B. "Lot sizes were small, and owners usually filled them up with cottages, barns, sheds, and outhouses…."
☐ C. "The city boasted having 59,500 buildings…large and ornately decorated."
☐ D. "…a closer inspection would reveal a wooden framework covered with cleverly painted copper or tin."

Question Four

Part A
In the introduction, the author states, "Chicago in 1871 was a city ready to burn." How does the author demonstrate this point?

○ A. He blames the middle-class and the poor for not knowing how to build a proper house.
○ B. He shows how Chicago's factories commonly ignored fire codes.
○ C. He describes how brick buildings were placed too close together.
○ D. He explains that wood was the primary building material.

Part B
What is an example from the text that supports your response to Part A?

☐ A. "It was also a common practice to disguise wood as another kind of building material."
☐ B. "Wealthier districts were by no means free of fire hazards."
☐ C. "Interspersed in these residential areas were a variety of businesses—paint factories, lumberyards, distilleries, gasworks, mills, furniture manufacturers, warehouses, and coal distributors."
☐ D. "The situation was worst in the middle-class and poorer districts."

Question Five

Part A
Sandburg and Murphy would both agree with which of the following statements about the city of Chicago?

○ A. Chicago looks like it is a strong city, but it has faults, too.
○ B. The people of Chicago are careless.
○ C. Chicago used to be a great industrial city, but that greatness is gone.
○ D. The lessons that we have learned from the Chicago fire are important.

Part B

Which statement from the texts supports your response to Part A? Select one response from each author.

- ☐ A. "Laughing even as an ignorant fighter laughs who has never lost a battle,"—Sandburg
- ☐ B. City of the Big Shoulders:/ They tell me you are wicked and I believe them, for I have seen your painted women under the gas lamps luring the farm boys."—Sandburg
- ☐ C. "The fancy exterior decorations on just about every building were carved from wood, then painted to look like stone or marble."—Murphy
- ☐ D. "Lot sizes were small, and owners usually filled them up with cottages, barns, sheds, and outhouses—all made of fast-burning wood, naturally."—Murphy

Essay Question

Directions: In "Chicago" and chapter one "A City Ready to Burn" from the book *The Great Fire*, the authors express different ideas about the city of Chicago. Write an essay that analyzes the authors' use of language to describe the city. Remember to use details from both texts to support your ideas.

PREWRITING SPACE
Use the space provided to make a writing plan for your essay.

Begin your essay here

Part Three

Narrative Task

50 minutes

Directions: Today, you will read from chapter six of novel *The Call of the Wild*, by Jack London. As you read, pay close attention to characterization, details, and conflict as you prepare to write a narrative story.

Please read the excerpt and answer the questions that accompany it.

Call of the Wild

by Jack London

It was brought about by a conversation in the Eldorado Saloon, in which men waxed boastful of their favorite dogs. Buck, because of his record, was the target for these men, and Thornton was driven stoutly to defend him. At the end of half an hour one man stated that his dog could start a sled with five hundred pounds and walk off with it; a second bragged six hundred for his dog; and a third, seven hundred.

"Pooh! pooh!" said John Thornton; "Buck can start a thousand pounds."

"And break it out? and walk off with it for a hundred yards?" demanded Matthewson, a Bonanza King, he of the seven hundred vaunt.

"And break it out, and walk off with it for a hundred yards," John Thornton said coolly.

"Well," Matthewson said, slowly and deliberately, so that all could hear, "I've got a thousand dollars that says he can't. And there it is." So saying, he slammed a sack of gold dust of the size of a bologna sausage down upon the bar….

The Eldorado emptied its occupants into the street to see the test. The tables were deserted, and the dealers and gamekeepers came forth to see the outcome of the wager and to lay odds. Several hundred men, furred and mittened, banked around the sled within easy distance. Matthewson's sled, loaded with a thousand pounds of flour, had been standing for a couple of hours, and in the intense cold (it was sixty below zero) the runners had frozen fast to the hard-packed snow. Men offered odds of two to one that Buck could not budge the sled. A quibble arose concerning the phrase "break out." O'Brien contended it was Thornton's privilege to knock the runners loose, leaving Buck to "break it out" from a dead standstill. Matthewson insisted that the phrase included breaking the runners from the frozen grip of the snow. A majority of the men who had witnessed the making of the bet decided in his favor, whereat the odds went up to three to one against Buck.

There were no takers. Not a man believed him capable of the feat. Thornton had been hurried into the wager, heavy with doubt; and now that he looked at the sled itself, the concrete fact, with the regular team of ten dogs curled up in the snow before it, the more impossible the task appeared. Matthewson waxed jubilant.

"Three to one!" he proclaimed. "I'll lay you another thousand at that figure, Thornton. What d'ye say?"

Thornton's doubt was strong in his face, but his fighting spirit was aroused—the fighting spirit that soars above odds, fails to recognize the impossible, and is deaf to all save the clamor for battle. He called Hans and Pete to him. Their sacks were slim, and with his own the three partners could rake together only two hundred dollars. In the ebb of their fortunes, this sum was their total capital; yet they laid it unhesitatingly against Matthewson's six hundred.

The team of ten dogs was unhitched, and Buck, with his own harness, was put into the sled. He had caught the contagion of the excitement, and he felt that in some way he must do a great thing for John Thornton. Murmurs of admiration at his splendid appearance went up. He was in perfect condition, without an ounce of superfluous flesh, and the one hundred and fifty pounds that he weighed were so many pounds of grit and virility. His furry coat shone with the sheen of silk. Down the neck and across the shoulders, his mane, in repose as it was, half bristled and seemed to lift with every movement, as though excess of vigor made each particular hair alive and active. The great breast and heavy fore legs were no more than in proportion with the rest of the body, where the muscles showed in tight rolls underneath the skin. Men felt these muscles and proclaimed them hard as iron, and the odds went down to two to one.

"Gad, sir! Gad, sir!" stuttered a member of the latest dynasty, a king of the Skookum Benches. "I offer you eight hundred for him, sir, before the test, sir; eight hundred just as he stands."

Thornton shook his head and stepped to Buck's side.

"You must stand off from him," Matthewson protested. "Free play and plenty of room."

The crowd fell silent; only could be heard the voices of the gamblers vainly offering two to one. Everybody acknowledged Buck a magnificent animal, but twenty fifty-pound sacks of flour bulked too large in their eyes for them to loosen their pouch-strings.

Thornton knelt down by Buck's side. He took his head in his two hands and rested cheek on cheek. He did not playfully shake him, as was his wont, or murmur soft love curses; but he whispered in his ear. "As you love me, Buck. As you love me," was what he whispered. Buck whined with suppressed eagerness.

The crowd was watching curiously. The affair was growing mysterious. It seemed like a conjuration. As Thornton got to his feet, Buck seized his mittened hand between his jaws, pressing in with his teeth and releasing slowly, half-reluctantly. It was the answer, in terms, not of speech, but of love. Thornton stepped well back.

"Now, Buck," he said.

Buck tightened the traces, then slacked them for a matter of several inches. It was the way he had learned.

"Gee!" Thornton's voice rang out, sharp in the tense silence.

Buck swung to the right, ending the movement in a plunge that took up the slack and with a sudden jerk arrested his one hundred and fifty pounds. The load quivered, and from under the runners arose a crisp crackling.

"Haw!" Thornton commanded.

Buck duplicated the manoeuvre, this time to the left. The crackling turned into a snapping, the sled pivoting and the runners slipping and grating several inches to the side. The sled was broken out. Men were holding their breaths, intensely unconscious of the fact.

Question One

Part A
Which of the choices below best expresses John Thornton's and Buck's relationship?

- ○ A. Buck is driven by fear to do things for Thornton.
- ○ B. Thornton is a kind owner who keeps Buck out of harm.
- ○ C. Thornton is a strict but kind master.
- ○ D. Buck loves Thornton and would do anything for him.

Part B

In the boxes below, please choose three details from the excerpt that support your selection for Part A.

1. 'As you love me, Buck. As you love me,' was what he whispered. Buck whined with suppressed eagerness."

2. 'Haw!' Thornton commanded."

3. "Pooh! pooh!" said John Thornton; 'Buck can start a thousand pounds.'

4. "Thornton knelt down by Buck's side. He took his head in his two hands and rested cheek on cheek."

5. "Thornton shook his head and stepped to Buck's side."

6. "'Gee!' Thornton's voice rang out, sharp in the tense silence."

7. "As Thornton got to his feet, Buck seized his mittened hand between his jaws, pressing in with his teeth and releasing slowly, half-reluctantly. It was the answer, in terms, not of speech, but of love."

Response One
Response Two
Response Three

Question Two

Part A

When John Thornton says, "As you love me, Buck. As you love me," what does that reveal about his relationship with Buck?

- ○ A. Thornton loves Buck and wishes he had not placed the bet.
- ○ B. He reminds Buck that Buck loves Thornton, showing the relationship is what Thornton gets from Buck, that Thornton is master and Buck the dog.
- ○ C. Buck expects just as much from Thornton as Thornton from Buck, and the words remind Buck that the relationship is about giving and taking.
- ○ D. Buck has betrayed Thornton in some way, and Thornton reminds Buck with the words so that Buck can make it up to him.

Part B

Which of the following statements best supports your choice for Part A?

- ○ A. Thornton does not say, "I love you." Instead, he whispers about Buck loving him.
- ○ B. Thornton knows Buck cannot pull the sled, but he is still going to let Buck try.
- ○ C. Buck knows he had done something wrong because Thornton "did not playfully shake him, as was his wont, or murmur soft love curses." That let Buck know that he had to make up for his mistake.
- ○ D. Thornton is a hard master, like when he yells, "'Gee!' Thornton's voice rang out, sharp in the tense silence."

Question Three

Part A

In the passage, the author states, "Not a man believed him capable of the feat. Thornton had been hurried into the wager, heavy with doubt; and now that he looked at the sled itself, the concrete fact, with the regular team of ten dogs curled up in the snow before it, the more impossible the task appeared." Why does Thornton still make the bet?

○ A. He has seen Buck pull a sled that heavy before.
○ B. He feels challenged and wants to win.
○ C. His partners, Hans and Pete, convince him that Buck can do it.
○ D. He knows he will lose but does not care.

Part B

Which explanation best supports your response to Part A?

○ A. Thornton knows from experience how much a dog can pull.
○ B. Thornton's partners are sure of Buck because they give Thornton all their money to make the bet.
○ C. Thornton is caught up in the moment and is blind to the realistic chances Buck has to do it.
○ D. John Thornton feels he can't back down from a bet even if he's sure to lose it.

Question Four

Part A

Thornton may be a good master in Buck's eyes, but what flaw does the author show about John Thornton?

○ A. John Thornton is not responsible handling money.
○ B. John Thornton is too close with an animal that pulls his sled.
○ C. On a selfish whim, John Thornton risks Buck for his pride and for money.
○ D. As a business partner, John Thornton is too controlling of Hans and Pete.

Part B

Which of the following choices best shows John Thornton's flaw?

○ A. "In the ebb of their fortunes, this sum was their total capital."
○ B. "He called Hans and Pete to him. Their sacks were slim, and with his own the three partners could rake together only two hundred dollars."
○ C. "Thornton shook his head and stepped to Buck's side."
○ D. "Pooh! pooh!" said John Thornton; "Buck can start a thousand pounds."

Question Five

Part A

The purpose of the article is to

○ A. inform the reader about the harshness of life in the Alaskan Gold Rush.

○ B. influence the reader into believing in bets with long odds.

○ C. entertain the reader with a dramatic story.

○ D. express the author's own life story.

Part B

Which of the following statements best supports your choice for Part A?

○ A. The passage uses words that make the reader think that taking a bet is a good idea.

○ B. Jack London, the author, uses accurate details that show what life was like in that setting, such as when he describes "Matthewson's sled, loaded with a thousand pounds of flour, had been standing for a couple of hours, and in the intense cold (it was sixty below zero) the runners had frozen fast to the hard-packed snow."

○ C. The text uses several dramatic instances, like "The load quivered, and from under the runners arose a crisp crackling."

○ D. The author's use of first person pronouns, such as "'Gad, sir! Gad, sir!'" stuttered a member of the latest dynasty, a king of the Skookum Benches. 'I offer you eight hundred for him, sir, before the test, sir; eight hundred just as he stands.'

Essay Question

Directions: In the passage, the author develops a situation with a bet over whether Buck, the sled dog, can pull a sled with a thousand pounds on it frozen in the snow. Think about the tension that the bet has created for Thorton, Buck's owner, Matthewson, who placed the bet, and for Buck himself. Write an original story to continue where the passage ended. In your story, be sure to use what you have learned about the situation as you tell what happens next.

PREWRITING SPACE
Use the space provided to make a writing plan for your essay.

Begin your essay here

Answers

Answers to the Research Simulation Task (Diners)

Question	Part A	Part B
1	C	2, 3, and 5
2	C	A
3	B	C
4	A	D
5	C	1 and 3
6	C	1, 6, and 8
7	B	A
8	Steinbeck: 6, 1 ADM: 2, 8	Both: 3, 9
9	Statements 3, 4, 5, 7, and 8	
10	C	C

Answers Explained

1. **Part A:** Choice C is the correct response. In the text, Steinbeck explains the trouble he has trying to observe people in New England towns because they are characteristically taciturn, or quiet.

   Part B: Details in 2, 3, and 5 explain Steinbeck's purpose in visiting the diner. Choice 1 is incorrect because it explains what he normally would do in a small town. Choice 4 is not correct because this is a general statement about people who rise early, not necessarily the men in the diner. Choice 6 explains how he got to that particular diner; choice 7 describes how the men in the diner were positioned.

2. **Part A:** Choice C is the correct response. As noted earlier, it means quiet.

   Part B: Choice A mentions that men "barely talk" to anyone. The other responses do not relate to being quiet.

3. **Part A:** Choice B is the correct response. As he traveled across the country collecting information about different populations, Steinbeck would "hold his peace." In other words, he would remain silent, so that he could eavesdrop on

conversations and thus gather intelligence about a town. However, when he is in New England, Steinbeck observed that the population is characteristically quiet. To learn anything about them, he needed to be in a place where they would chat, so that he could remain silent and observe.

Part B: Choice C is the correct response because it is a shorter explanation of what was just described in the reasoning for Part A.

4. **Part A:** Choice A is the correct response because it is the only response actually mentioned in the text. None of the other scenarios occur.

   Part B: Choice D is the correct response; it provides a commentary on the conversation between the waitress and the customer.

5. **Part A:** Choice C is the correct answer as it defines what the term "greasy spoon" means; a restaurant that is not maintained and therefore not too popular. The sentence before the term implies that the diner owners were not taking good care of their establishments. Although the sentence after it makes an assertion that because some diners' reputations were not good (not clean), many criminals began to gather there, choice B is not correct. Just because a restaurant is not clean does not automatically mean there are criminals in it. There might be less people in the restaurant.

   Part B: A greasy spoon is not maintained. Going on that premise, the opposite of neglect would be to take extra care of the restaurant. Choice 1 describes fancy woodwork and stained glass, therefore, that is one of the correct choices. Choice 3 is also correct. It explains that diners were popular because they offered inexpensive meals and were open after 8pm.

6. **Part A:** Choice C is the correct response. An icon is a symbol.

   Part B: Statements 1, 6, and 8 support choice C for Part A as they provide consistent descriptions of this symbol.

7. **Part A:** Choice B is correct; the author's purpose is to provide a history of the diner phenomenon. Look at the subheadings: **What is a Diner?**, **How Diners Began**, and **Over the Decades**.

   Part B: Choice A is correct. It explains the progression of the article as outlined in the explanation for Part A.

8. Steinbeck 1, 6; American Diner Museum 2, 8; Both: 3, 9.

   Statement 1: As Steinbeck is trying to gather information about the community, he is compelled to go to a diner when a bar and a church are not available to him. It is the only place people gather every day.

Statement 2: This statement is the summary of one of the main points in the American Diner Museum article.

Statement 3: Both texts discuss diners in New England.

Statement 4: Neither text says this. In fact, Steinbeck contradicts this as he notes that the diner is only place available to him as a "wayfaring stranger."

Statement 5: This is not supported or implied by either article.

Statement 6: Steinbeck notes that this is the only time that he knows people will be at the diner. The American Diner Museum says the opposite; diners were popular because they were open late.

Statement 7: This is not supported or implied by either article.

Statement 8: The American Diner Museum describes the popularity of "Nite Owls."

Statement 9: This is depicted in both texts.

9. Statements 3, 4, 5, 7, and 8 are the correct choices.

Statement 1: The painting is clearly at night. No one is going hunting.

Statement 2: Again, the painting is entitled "Night Hawks" because it is night.

Statement 3: All of the customers are seated at the counter. The diner is the only business on the street with its lights on.

Statement 4: Each customer leans over a cup of coffee.

Statement 5: A counter, stools, and food preparation area are present in the painting.

Statement 6: This statement has nothing to do with the painting.

Statement 7: The painting depicts a diner at night.

Statement 8: The painting depicts a diner at night.

10. **Part A:** Choice C is correct. The painting is entitled "Nighthawks." There is nothing to indicate that they have been at work (briefcases, tools, etc.) so choice A is not correct. Although the street is empty, no evidence suggests that it is cold outside (no hats, scarves, snow, frost, etc.); therefore, B is not correct. Choice D seems like a stretch. The best choice is C.

Part B: Choice C is correct. It provides the best description of what is actually is shown in the painting.

Sample Essay: Score 4

Last Sunday, my family celebrated my grandfather's birthday. He could have chosen any restaurant to celebrate his seventieth birthday, but he chose his favorite meal at his favorite restaurant: brunch at our town's diner. As the hostess escorted us past the glass case of desserts to our table, we passed by the counter with its shiny stools occupied by old men silently sipping coffee. That quiet section in the diner is one that is familiar to many Americans. Through the years, the diner has served Americans more than cups of coffee. The American diner is a symbol of the service industry because it has always catered to its customers' needs.

One of the most important things that diner customers need is a clean, comfortable place to eat. Although some diners have had a reputation for being a greasy spoon (Source B), most diners have offered customers clean accommodations as depicted in "Nighthawks." In the painting, the waiter has a clean, white uniform and serves the customers coffee from shining silver cylinders. Diner owners also attempted to make their establishments enticing by putting a fancy finish on a dining car; Source B discusses how some diners were "elaborate and were fitted with stained and etched glass windows, intricately painted murals and fancy woodwork."

Diners also define the service industry simply by being open when other restaurants are not. The first diners began as a result of Walter Scott noticing an opportunity to serve food to a population that worked too late to go to a restaurant (Source B). Sometimes, diners were even called "Nite Owls" because they were open so late (Source B). Nearly eighty-five years later, Hopper's painting depicts the same quality of the diner in "Nighthawk."; the diner is open and serving customers so late at night that there is no one on the street outside.

"Open when other restaurants are not" does not strictly mean that diners are only open late at night; many diners are open early in the morning, way before other restaurants owners even think about opening their doors. Steinbeck noticed this while he was writing "Travels with Charley," and he went into a diner early in the morning to observe the customers. What he found was similar to what is depicted in "Nighthawks," people sitting on a stool quietly drinking a cup of coffee.

While he is in the diner, Steinbeck describes what he calls a typical conversation between a waitress and a customer. Although Steinbeck pokes fun of the interaction between the two, the dialogue that he records between the two illustrates how the wait staff at diners know what their customers want. Steinbeck notes, "Early-rising men not only do not talk much to strangers, they barely talk to one another. Breakfast conversation is limited to a series of laconic grunts." Because the waitress knows this, she makes a little friendly conversation with him, which is what he wants because it is early, and pours him another cup of coffee, which he wants because it's cold outside.

Diners are so much more than a place to grab a cup of coffee. They are clean, comfortable establishments that offer friendly service any time of day—or night. Because diners make us feel so at home, their role as a symbol of the American service industry is unequalled.

This essay would earn a 4, or full credit, on the PARCC's draft rubric. It demonstrates that the student has a clear understanding of all of the texts and was able to incorporate more than one into her response. The introductory paragraph is an interesting personal anecdote. The author does an excellent job synthesizing information from two or more sources, best exemplified in body paragraph three. The logic that the author uses is based in the evidence that goes across the texts. The essay is well-organized: there is a clear introductory paragraph with a thesis, supporting evidence, transitions between paragraphs, and a concluding paragraph with a restatement of the thesis. The author uses a quote to make a transition, "Open when others are not…." The author maintains a formal style to appropriately address the readers, and it is evident that he had time to proofread his response as there are no grammatical errors.

Answers to the Literary Analysis Task (Chicago)

Question	Part A	Part B
1	C	C, D
2	C	A, D
3	D	A
4	C	A, D
5	A	B, C

Answers Explained

1. **Part A:** Choice C is correct. Sandburg calls the city Hog Butcher, Tool Maker, Wheat Stacker, and Freight Handler.

   Part B: Choices C and D are correct. At the conclusion of the poem, Sandburg restates the jobs to put emphasis on the city's working class identity (Choice C). He personifies the city as a working man and goes as far to describe him as a "youth" who is "half-naked, sweating, proud to be the Hog Butcher...." (Choice D).

2. **Part A:** Choice C is correct because Sandburg says although the city has problems, it also has great things, like people who work hard.

   Part B: Choices A and D are correct. Both of these choices reinforce the idea of the city as a working man.

3. **Part A:** Choice C is correct. The construction looked like it was sturdy and could survive much, but in reality, it simply wasn't.

   Part B: Choices A and D are correct. The idea that Murphy expresses is that everything was wood, which would burn. These two choices identify that wood was hidden in the construction of every building.

4. **Part A:** Choice D is correct. Throughout the article, Murphy explains that because everything was wooden, the city was ready to burn.

   Part B: Choice A is correct as it explains that although construction appeared to not be wood, it actually was as it was a common practice to disguise the wood as another material.

5. **Part A:** Choice A is correct. The two authors do not agree about much, but they would agree that this strong, industrial city has faults.

   Part B: Choices B and C are correct. Both of these quotes acknowledge that something is amiss in Chicago.

Sample Essay: Score 4

If you said the words "Chicago Fire" to someone today, that person might tell you that "Chicago Fire" is a television show. But if you had an opportunity to talk with Jim Murphy or Carl Sandburg, they would each say something different about that topic. Murphy would talk about how a fire, caused primarily by shoddily built wooden structures, burned Chicago to the ground. In contrast, Sandburg might discuss how the industrious people of Chicago had a fire in their bellies. However different their ideas might be, Murphy and Sandburg both used comparison and catalogue to create images of Chicago.

Although they have very different opinions about the city, both of the authors used comparison to depict the city. As he makes his point about which areas of Chicago are the most flammable, Murphy compares one area of Chicago to another. For example, he says in the second paragraph, "The situation was worst in the middle-class and poorer districts"; then in the third paragraph, he offers the comparison to the wealthier districts, adding that they weren't that much safer. He also states that many of the larger buildings were made of wood but painted to give the impression that they were marble. The overall impression is that the city is ready to spark at any second, and that spark could be set anywhere in town.

Murphy's depiction of Chicago is a criticism of how the city was built. In the poem, Sandburg addresses other critics of Chicago by acknowledging the negative things they've said. He then challenges these critics when he says, "Come and show me another city with lifted head singing\so proud to be alive and coarse and strong and cunning.\Flinging magnetic curses amid the toil of piling job on\job, here is a tall bold slugger set vivid against the\little soft cities." There are two comparisons in that quotation. Sandburg calls other cities "soft" which implies that Chicago is "hard" or "tough." Sandburg uses a metaphor to compare Chicago to a fighter who is cursing and singing as he works.

In addition to comparisons made in the texts, both authors use catalogue to depict the city. In his description of the layout of the city, Murphy says, "Interspersed in these residential areas were a variety of businesses—paint factories, lumberyards, distilleries, gasworks, mills, furniture manufacturers, warehouses, and coal distributors." Similarly, Sandburg uses catalogue to depict Chicago's industry with the names he calls the city at the beginning and the end of the poem, "proud to be Hog\Butcher, Tool Maker, Stacker of Wheat, Player with\ Railroads and Freight Handler to the Nation." The effect of this use of figurative language in both texts is that the reader has a clear sense of the type of work that the people of Chicago did.

Murphy and Sandburg might debate the quality of the work accomplished in the city, but they would definitely agree that their depictions of Chicago are ones that reflect a city of people who work. The use of catalogue details the work that was accomplished, and the authors' use of comparison describes how sections of the city were divided between industry and residence, shows how Chicago compares to other cities, and provides a very human image of the city itself.

This essay would earn a 4, or full credit, on the PARCC's draft rubric. This is a challenging essay to write because there is seemingly little in common with each essay other than the city of Chicago. The author of the essay recognizes that Sandburg and Murphy describe the qualities of work about the city, and he resolves the conflicting points of view in the introduction by bringing in a recent television show, *Chicago Fire*. The conflict resolution is further resolved in the second paragraph. The essay is well-organized: there is a clear introductory paragraph with a thesis, supporting evidence, transitions between paragraphs, and a concluding paragraph with a restatement of the thesis. The author maintains a formal style to appropriately address the readers, and it is evident that he had time to proofread his response as there are no grammatical errors.

Answers to Narrative Task (The Call of the Wild)

Question	Part A	Part B
1	D	Choices 1, 4, and 7
2	B	A
3	B	C
4	C	D
5	C	C

Answers Explained

1. **Part A:** D is the correct answer. Buck loves Thornton so much that he pulls a heavy sled for him.

    Part B: 1,4, and 7 are the correct answers. Since we know from Part A that Buck loves Thornton and would do anything for him, these answers must show that. Choice 1 speaks of Buck's love for Thornton. Choice 4 shows a loving moment when master and dog hug. Choice 7 again shows Buck holding Thornton's hand in his mouth lovingly. Because all three choices show Buck's love for Thornton, all three are correct.

2. **Part A:** B is the correct answer. Thornton does not say that he loves Buck. Instead, he tells Buck that Buck loves him. This shows that Thornton is the master and Buck is his dog.

    Part B: A is the correct answer. Since the answer to Part A is about Thornton telling Buck that Buck loves him, Choice A explains what Thornton does not say ("I love you").

3. **Part A:** B is the correct answer. The key words to let the reader know that Thornton feels challenged but still wants to win are "Thornton had been hurried into the wager." This shows that he got caught up in the moment.

    Part B: C is the correct answer. The "hurried into the wager" citation shows how he is caught up in the moment, and now that he sees the task, "the more impossible the task appeared" shows that he was blind to Buck's chances.

4. **Part A:** C is the correct answer. Thornton and Buck care for each other, but Thornton, without much thought, places a bet that Buck can pull a huge load through the ice. This whim shows a flaw in Thornton.

Part B: D is the correct answer. Thornton's boast that Buck can start a thousand pounds shows that he puts little thought into placing Buck in harm's way on just a bet.

5. **Part A:** C is the correct answer. Entertaining stories show dialogue, drama, and suspense, and this passage from *The Call of the Wild* has these elements. It is meant to entertain.

   Part B: C is the correct answer. It specifically mentions the word *dramatic*, and it gives an example of a suspenseful moment.

Sample Essay: Score 4

"He'll never do it!" Matthewson cried.

But Buck started to his side again, his paws slipping on the snow that had packed into a solid layer of ice. Once Buck slipped and fell, and again the men in the crowd unconsciously held their breath.

Buck lay for a moment, feeling the cold of the frozen ground against his belly, the minus sixty stabbing at him through his thick fur. He put one front paw below him then the other, and then deliberately rose front first. He repeated the process with his back legs and heard the crowd let out a collective sigh.

"Haw!" Thornton commanded again.

Buck knew he must do this great thing for John Thornton, and he fixed his gaze down the road. He felt the harness tighten, and again, he swung from side to side. This time the sled broke free and clear of the ice, and it moved five feet before Buck's feet slipped out from beneath him. But Buck knew he could not fall again, and he caught himself before he went down.

Here the road started a slight downhill slope, and this made it easier for Buck.

"He's going to do it!" Hans cried.

"Go, Buck! Go!" Pete called.

The end was in sight. Matthewson walked the whole stretch alongside Buck, keeping his eyes fixed on Buck's feet as they struggled to grip the ice. But the end was in sight. It lay a few yards ahead.

The last few yards down the road from The Eldorado had a great change in the slope, and neither Thornton nor Buck knew that this hill was there. Buck, feeling his confidence grow, pulled faster now, but when the sled hit the crest of the hill, the enormous weight it carried propelled it forward.

Buck felt the weight fall from his harness. He looked back to see the sled bearing down on him. Buck tried to sidestep the sled, but it was too late. The sled smashed down hard into Buck from behind, knocking him alongside the sled, and then, once it passed, the sled pulled Buck, still in the harness, across the finish line.

The crowd's cheer went as fast as it came as John Thornton rushed to Buck's side.

"No wager," Matthewson said, ignoring Buck's whimper. "Your dog did not pull the sled the whole distance."

Thornton ignored him. The bet did not matter anymore. "Keep the gold," he said. He brushed Buck's face with his mittened hand. "I see what it's worth."

The crowd had gathered around Mattewson. "Give it to him!" someone called.

Matthewson refused. "No. He didn't complete it."

John Thornton took Buck into his arms, cheek to cheek. "As I love you," he said. "As I love you."

Hans and Pete broke through the crowd. "The nearest anyone can help is in Yellowknife," Hans said. "It's ten miles."

John Thornton kicked the flour sacks out of the sled and laid Buck on its bottom. "I'll take him."

"But we can't gather the team of dogs in time," Pete said.

"No," Thornton said. "I did this. I will take him."

With that, John Thornton put his shoulders in the harness. Again the crowd held a collective breath. Buck felt the sled again break from the ice and start down the road again. This time, though, he was riding in it, not pulling it. He looked ahead and saw John Thornton's back in the harness, heading down the road into the dark of night. Again he whimpered, not out of pain but out of love for this man.

This essay would earn a 4, or full credit, on the PARCC's draft rubric. It demonstrates that the student has a clear understanding of the story and has continued the tale by using the dialogue, style, and vocabulary choices in the original text. The events that the student response presents are logically connected with the rest of London's story.

Practice Test— End-of-Year Assessment

Practice the PARCC End-of-Year Assessment

Now it is time to try an EOY on your own. Time yourself as you take the assessment. The answer keys are at the end of each section of the EOY.

Part One

Reading Comprehension

70 minutes

Directions: The Middle Passage is the route that many enslaved Africans were transported from Africa to the Americas. The conditions upon the ships that carried slaves were deplorable. Many of the anti-slavery activists, abolitionists, used examples of the treatment of slaves on the plantation as well as the Middle Passage as reasons for abolishing slavery.

Today, you will read about how slaves were treated by reading an African-American folk tale and reading an excerpt from an autobiography. As you read, you will respond to questions about each text. The last two questions will ask you about both texts.

"The People Could Fly"
Virginia Hamilton

They say the people could fly. Say that long ago in Africa, some of the people knew magic. And they would walk up on the air like climbin' up on a gate. And they flew like blackbirds over the fields. Black, shiny wings flappin' against the blue up there.

Then, many of the people were captured for Slavery. The ones that could fly shed their wings. They couldn't take their wings across the water on slave ships. Too crowded, don't you know.

The folks were full of misery, then. Got sick with the up and down of the sea. So they forgot about flyin' when they could no longer breathe the sweet scent of Africa.

Say the people who could fly kept their power, although they shed their wings. They looked the same as the other people from Africa who had been coming over, who had dark skin. Say you couldn't tell anymore one who could fly from one who couldn't.

One such who could was an old man, call him Toby. And standin' tall, yet afraid, was a young woman who once had wings. Call her Sarah. Now Sarah carried a babe tied to her back. She trembled to be so hard worked and scorned.

The slaves labored in the fields from sunup to sundown. The owner of the slaves callin' himself their Master. Say he was a hard lump of clay. A hard, glinty coal. A hard rock pile, wouldn't be moved. His Overseer on horseback pointed out the slaves who were slowin' down. So the one called Driver cracked his whip over the slow ones to make them move faster. That whip was a slice-open cut of pain. So they did move faster. Had to.

Sarah hoed and chopped the row as the babe on her back slept.

Say the child grew hungry. That babe started up bawling too loud. Sarah couldn't stop to feed it. Couldn't stop to soothe and quiet it down. She let it cry. She didn't want to. She had no heart to croon to it.

"Keep that thing quiet," called the Overseer. He pointed his finger at the babe. The woman scrunched low. The Driver cracked his whip across the babe anyhow. The babe hollered like any hurt child, and the woman fell to the earth.

The old man that was there, Toby, came and helped her to her feet. "I must go soon," she told him.

"Soon," he said.

Sarah couldn't stand up straight any longer. She was too weak. The sun burned her face. The babe cried and cried, "Pity me, oh, pity me," say it sounded like. Sarah was so sad and starvin', she sat down in the row.

"Get up, you black cow," called the Overseer. He pointed his hand, and the Driver's whip snarled around Sarah's legs. Her sack dress tore into rags. Her legs bled onto the earth. She couldn't get up.

Toby was there where there was no one to help her and the babe.

"Now before it's too late," panted Sarah."Now, Father!"

"Yes, Daughter, the time is come," Toby answered. Go, as you know how to go!"

He raised his arms, holding them out to her.

"*Kum...yali, kum buba tambe,*" and more magic words, said so quickly, they sounded like whispers and sighs.

The young woman lifted one foot on the air. Then the other. She flew clumsily at first, with the child now held tightly in her arms. Then she felt the magic, the African mystery. Say she rose just as free as a bird. As light as a feather.

The Overseer rode after her, hollerin'. Sarah flew over the fences. She flew over the woods. Tall trees could not snag her. Nor could the Overseer. She flew like an eagle now, until she was gone from sight. No one dared speak about it. Couldn't believe it. But it was, because they that was there saw that it was.

Another and another fell from the heat. Toby was there. He cried out to the fallen and reached his arms out to them. "*Kum kunka yali, kum...tambe!*" Whispers and sighs. And they too rose on the air. They rode the hot breezes. The ones flyin' were black and shinin' sticks, wheelin' above the head of the Overseer. They crossed the rows, the fields, the fences, the streams, and were away.

"Seize the old man!" cried the Overseer. "I heard him say the magic words. Seize him!"

The one callin' himself Master come runnin'. The Driver got his whip ready to curl around old Toby and tie him up. The slave owner took his hip gun from its place. He meant to kill old black Toby.

But Toby just laughed Say he threw back his head and said, "Hee, hee! Don't you know who I am? Don't you know some of us in this field?" He said it to their faces. "We are ones who fly!" And he sighed the ancient words that were a dark promise. He said them all around to the other in the field under the whip, "*...buba yali...buba tambe...*"

There was a great outcryin'. The bent backs straighten up. Old and young who were called slaves and could fly joined hands. Say like they would ring-sing. But they didn't shuffle in a circle. They didn't sing. They rose on the air. They flew in a flock that was black against the heavenly blue. Black crows or black shadows. It didn't matter, they went so high. Way above the plantation, way over the slavery land. Say they flew away to Free-dom.

And the old man, old Toby, flew behind them, takin' care of them. He wasn't cryin'. He wasn't laughin'. He was the seer. His faze fell on the plantation where the slave who could not fly waited.

"Take us with you!" Their looks spoke it, but they were afraid to shout it. Toby couldn't take them with him. Hadn't the time to teach them to fly. They must wait for a chance to run.

"Goodie-bye!" the old man called Toby spoke to them, poor souls! And he was flyin' gone. So they say. The Overseer told it. The one called Master said it was a lie, a trick of the light. The Driver kept his mouth shut.

The slaves who could not fly told about the people who could fly to their children. When they were free. When they sat close before the fire in the free land, they told it. They did so love firelight and Free-dom, and tellin'.

They say that the children of the ones who could not fly told their children. And now, me, I have told it to you.

Question One

Part A

Most folk tales are intended to be read aloud. What rhetorical technique does the author use to create the sense that the story was once read aloud?

○ A. alliteration
○ B. dialogue
○ C. transcription of incantations
○ D. spelling words as they sound

Part B

What is an example of the rhetorical device that you chose?

○ A. "Now before it's too late," panted Sarah."Now, Father!" "Yes, Daughter, the time is come," Toby answered. Go, as you know how to go!"
○ B. "The ones flyin' were black and shinin' sticks, wheelin' above the head of the Overseer."
○ C. The bent backs straighten up.
○ D. *"Kum kunka yali, kum...tambe!"*

Question Two

Part A

Which of the following offers the best explanation that Hamilton capitalized the words "Driver," "Overseer," and "Master"?

○ A. Those words are being used as names for the characters in the tale.
○ B. The author does not know their names so uses those as names.
○ C. Those three men are evil so they do not get individual names like Toby and Sarah do.
○ D. There is really only one man, but the slaves view him as having three different personalities.

Part B

Which one of these is NOT an accurate description of the Driver, Overseer, or Master?

○ A. He does what he is told without consideration for the people laboring in the field.
○ B. He makes promises to people that he cannot keep.
○ C. He is not really available until there is trouble.
○ D. He seems to be everywhere, all of the time, and directs everything.

Question Three

Part A
What irony exists in the interaction between the Driver, the Overseer, Sarah, and the babe?

- ○ A. Sarah and the babe have the power to fly, and not knowing this, the Driver and Overseer ask her to fly away.
- ○ B. They don't know that Toby is Sarah's father. When the Overseer asks Sarah to keep the baby quiet, the person he should be addressing is Toby so that he can keep Sarah, his "babe", from talking back to the Overseer and Driver.
- ○ C. If they let her rest, she could feed and soothe the baby. The Driver strikes her and the baby, and the Overseer tells her to keep it quiet. Babies don't become quiet when they are hit.
- ○ D. The Driver and Overseer care a lot about Sarah and her baby because they realize that the baby will eventually grow up to be another slave. The Driver attempts to calm the baby down, but does not know how to use anything but a whip.

Part B
As Sarah flies away, the author says:

> The young woman lifted one foot on the air. Then the other. She flew clumsily at first, with the child now held tightly in her arms. Then she felt the magic, the African mystery. Say she rose just as free as a bird. As light as a feather.
>
> The Overseer rode after her, hollerin'. Sarah flew over the fences. She flew over the woods. Tall trees could not snag her. Nor could the Overseer. She flew like an eagle now, until she was gone from sight. No one dared speak about it. Couldn't believe it. But it was, because they that was there saw that it was.

What literary device is primarily used in this excerpt?

- ○ A. simile
- ○ B. onomatopoeia
- ○ C. conceit
- ○ D. alliteration

Question Four

Part A

How is Toby contrasted with the Overseer?

- ○ A. The Overseer has power given to him by the Master, but Toby has supernatural powers from Africa.
- ○ B. The Overseer cannot see or hear Toby, but Toby can see and hear everything that the Overseer does.
- ○ C. The Overseer has no power over Toby, but Toby can say magic words and curse the Overseer.
- ○ D. The Overseer has to work with the Driver to have people respect him, but Toby has people respect him because he can fly.

Part B

Why does the author say that Toby could not take everyone in his flight?

- ○ A. If Toby took everyone, there would be no one to work on the plantation, and the Master, Driver, and Overseer would have nothing to do but chase the escaped slaves.
- ○ B. If Toby took everyone, there would not be anyone to observe him, tell the story of his flight, and pass the story down through the generations.
- ○ C. It's not that Toby didn't want to take everyone on his flight, it's that there were too many people to teach how to fly at once and Toby couldn't be bothered with that task.
- ○ D. Toby only selected those who were ready to go with him. He left behind the people who made fun of him, called him "old," and took his food.

This excerpt is from Chapter V of *The Interesting Narrative of the Life of Olaudah Equiano* by Olaudah Equiano. Obtained from The Gutenberg Project at http://www.gutenberg.org/zipcat2. php/15399/15399-h/15399-h.htm

The Interesting Narrative of the Life of Olaudah Equiano

Olaudah Equiano

In this state of my mind our ship came to an anchor, and soon after discharged her cargo. I now knew what it was to work hard; I was made to help to unload and load the ship. And, to comfort me in my distress in that time, two of the sailors robbed me of all my money, and ran away from the ship. I had been so long used to a European climate that at first I felt the scorching West India sun very painful, while the dashing surf would toss the boat and the people in it frequently above high water mark. Sometimes our limbs were broken with this, or even attended with instant death, and I was day by day mangled and torn.

About the middle of May, when the ship was got ready to sail for England, I all the time believing that Fate's blackest clouds were gathering over my head, and expecting their bursting would mix me with the dead, Captain Doran sent for me ashore one morning, and I was told by the messenger that my fate was then determined. With fluttering steps and trembling heart I came to the captain, and found with him one Mr. Robert King, a quaker, and the first merchant in the place. The captain then told me my former master had sent me there to be sold; but that he had desired him to get me the best master he could, as he told him I was a very deserving boy, which Captain Doran said he found to be true; and if he were to stay in the West Indies he would be glad to keep me himself; but he could not venture to take me to London, for he was very sure that when I came there I would leave him. I at that instant burst out a crying, and begged much of him to take me to England with him, but all to no purpose. He told me he had got me the very best master in the whole island, with whom I should be as happy as if I were in England, and for that reason he chose to let him have me, though he could sell me to his own brother-in-law for a great deal more money than what he got from this gentleman. Mr. King, my new master, then made a reply, and said the reason he had bought me was on account of my good character; and, as he had not the least doubt of my good behaviour, I should be very well off with him. He also told me he did not live in the West Indies, but at

Philadelphia, where he was going soon; and, as I understood something of the rules of arithmetic, when we got there he would put me to school, and fit me for a clerk. This conversation relieved my mind a little, and I left those gentlemen considerably more at ease in myself than when I came to them; and I was very grateful to Captain Doran, and even to my old master, for the character they had given me; a character which I afterwards found of infinite service to me….Mr. King soon asked me what I could do; and at the same time said he did not mean to treat me as a common slave. I told him I knew something of seamanship, and could shave and dress hair pretty well; and I could refine wines, which I had learned on shipboard, where I had often done it; and that I could write, and understood arithmetic tolerably well ….

My master was several times offered by different gentlemen one hundred guineas for me; but he always told them he would not sell me, to my great joy: and I used to double my diligence and care for fear of getting into the hands of those men who did not allow a valuable slave the common support of life. Many of them even used to find fault with my master for feeding his slaves so well as he did; although I often went hungry, and an Englishman might think my fare very indifferent; but he used to tell them he always would do it, because the slaves thereby looked better and did more work.

Question Five

Part A
Equiano states, "I was day by day mangled and torn." How has this happened to him?

- ○ A. His master whipped him and made him work hard.
- ○ B. Two sailors robbed him and beat him up.
- ○ C. He was overheated and tossed about the ship in rough seas.
- ○ D. He was kept in a passage that also held the dead.

Part B

What evidence from the text supports your answer for Part A?

1	"And, to comfort me in my distress in that time, two of the sailors robbed me of all my money, and ran away from the ship."
2	"I had been so long used to an European climate that at first I felt the scorching West India sun very painful, while the dashing surf would toss the boat and the people in it frequently above high water mark."
3	"In this state of my mind our ship came to an anchor, and soon after discharged her cargo. I now knew what it was to work hard; I was made to help to unload and load the ship."
4	"… expecting their bursting would mix me with the dead, Captain Doran sent for me ashore one morning, and I was told by the messenger that my fate was then determined."
5	"I at that instant burst out a crying, and begged much of him to take me to England with him, but all to no purpose."
6	"…as he told him I was a very deserving boy, which Captain Doran said he found to be true; and if he were to stay in the West Indies he would be glad to keep me himself…."

Question Six

Part A

All three of the following claims about the mistreatment of slaves are present in the excerpt. Please select the one that an abolitionist would use as his strongest argument.

Claim One	Slaves worked hard in dangerous conditions and were poorly treated.
Claim Two	Slaves were poorly fed but were taught skills in a variety of trades.
Claim Three	Masters showed little regard for how slaves were treated.

Part B

Select three pieces of evidence from the list that would support the claim you chose for Part A.

1	"In this state of my mind our ship came to an anchor, and soon after discharged her cargo. I now knew what it was to work hard; I was made to help to unload and load the ship."
2	"He also told me he did not live in the West Indies, but at Philadelphia, where he was going soon; and, as I understood something of the rules of arithmetic, when we got there he would put me to school, and fit me for a clerk."
3	"Mr. King soon asked me what I could do; and at the same time said he did not mean to treat me as a common slave."
4	"I at that instant burst out a crying, and begged much of him to take me to England with him, but all to no purpose."
5	"I used to double my diligence and care for fear of getting into the hands of those men who did not allow a valuable slave the common support of life."
6	"Many of them even used to find fault with my master for feeding his slaves so well as he did; although I often went hungry, and an Englishman might think my fare very indifferent; but he used to tell them he always would do it, because the slaves thereby looked better and did more work."
7	"The captain then told me my former master had sent me there to be sold; but that he had desired him to get me the best master he could, as he told him I was a very deserving boy, which Captain Doran said he found to be true;…."
8	"Sometimes our limbs were broken with this, or even attended with instant death…"
9	"…for the character they had given me; a character which I afterwards found of infinite service to me…."

Question Seven

Part A
Why did Captain Doran select a specific buyer for Equiano?

- ○ A. Doran wanted to make sure that he actually went to the West Indies instead of returning to England.
- ○ B. Doran wanted to keep Equiano for himself or at least send him to his brother-in-law.
- ○ C. Doran was instructed by Equiano's previous master to send Equiano to school, so he wanted to ensure that whoever bought him would see that he received an education.
- ○ D. Doran was told by Equiano's previous master that Equiano was good, so he wanted to make sure that he was treated well.

Part B
What evidence from the text supports your response for Part A?

- ○ A. The captain then told me my former master had sent me there to be sold; but that he had desired him to get me the best master he could, as he told him I was a very deserving boy, which Captain Doran said he found to be true; and if he were to stay in the West Indies he would be glad to keep me himself; but he could not venture to take me to London, for he was very sure that when I came there I would leave him.
- ○ B. This conversation relieved my mind a little, and I left those gentlemen considerably more at ease in myself than when I came to them; and I was very grateful to Captain Doran, and even to my old master, for the character they had given me; a character which I afterwards found of infinite service to me.
- ○ C. My master was several times offered by different gentlemen one hundred guineas for me; but he always told them he would not sell me, to my great joy: and I used to double my diligence and care for fear of getting into the hands of those men who did not allow a valuable slave the common support of life.
- ○ D. He told me he had got me the very best master in the whole island, with whom I should be as happy as if I were in England, and for that reason he chose to let him have me, though he could sell me to his own brother-in-law for a great deal more money than what he got from this gentleman.

Question Eight

Part A

At various points in this excerpt there are ellipses. What is the function of this punctuation?

- ○ A. Ellipses are used to abbreviate larger words.
- ○ B. Ellipses are used to shorten longer portions of text.
- ○ C. Ellipses are used to indicate the passage of time.
- ○ D. Ellipses are used to change the subject.

Part B

Why does Equiano use both capital and lowercase letters for the two appearances of the word *fate* in the following sentence?

> About the middle of May, when the ship was got ready to sail for England, I all the time believing that Fate's blackest clouds were gathering over my head, and expecting their bursting would mix me with the dead, Captain Doran sent for me ashore one morning, and I was told by the messenger that my fate was then determined.

- ○ A. The capital letter reveals Equiano's concern about what will happen to him, and the lower case letter indicates he is happy with what has been decided for him.
- ○ B. Both the capital letter and the lower case letter indicate that Equiano does not really care about where he goes because he feels that he is property.
- ○ C. In the beginning of the sentence, the Fate is personified; at the end of the sentence, Equiano knows his personal situation.
- ○ D. The capital letter indicates that events were beyond his control; the lower case letter indicates that Equiano would determine what would happen when he reach the West Indies.

Question Nine

Part A

Which of the following images is present in both texts?

- ○ A. black birds flying high into the air
- ○ B. the rough seas
- ○ C. black clouds against a blue sky
- ○ D. the green fields of the plantation

Part B

How are the masters depicted in the texts?

○ **A.** In the folk tale, the master commands many people and gets them to work hard by whipping them. In the autobiography, the master feeds the slaves well so that they will work hard for him.

○ **B.** In the folk tale, the master only treats the slaves well when he realizes they can fly. In the autobiography, the master puts the slaves to work on the ship without regard for their well-being.

○ **C.** In the folk tale, the master treats the slaves kindly even though his overseer and driver mistreat the slaves. In the autobiography, the master mistreats the slaves until he realizes that they can read, write, and do arithmetic.

○ **D.** In the folk tale, the master frequently beats the slaves. In the autobiography, the master pays the slaves so that they can buy their freedom.

Question Ten

Both of the authors depict the difficult life that slaves led, but the intended audiences and purpose for each text is different. Drag and drop your choices for the audience, purpose, and your justification of each text from the first chart into the second.

Choices for Audience, Purpose, and Justification		
Audience	**Purpose**	**Justification**
Slave owners	To enlighten and entertain	There are examples in this text that are worded as if they are a law.
African-Americans	To demonstrate how slaves were bought and sold	This text demonstrates that people could escape slavery and enjoy freedom.
Americans who wanted to end slavery	To justify the passing of a law	This text mentions the slave trade in Europe and in America.
The U.S. government	To show how children of slaves were treated	There are many mentions in this text about the purchase of slaves.
Europeans	To provide hope	This text demonstrates the difference between being a "good" and "poor" slave owner.

Text	Audience	Purpose	Justification
"The People Could Fly"			
The Interesting Narrative of Olaudah Equiano			

Answers

Question	Part A	Part B
1	D	B
2	A	B
3	C	A
4	A	B
5	C	2
6	Claim 1	1,5, and 8
7	D	A
8	B	C
9	B	A
10	"The People Could Fly" Audience: African-Americans Purpose: To provide hope Justification: This text demonstrates that people could escape and enjoy freedom.	*The Interesting Narrative of Olaudah Equiano* Audience: Americans who wanted to end slavery Purpose: To demonstrate how slaves were bought and sold. Justification: There are many mentions in this text about the purchase of slaves.

Answers Explained

1. **Part A:** Choice D is correct. The words are spelled as the characters may have pronounced them.

   Part B: Choice B is correct. The author leaves off the "g" sound in flying, shining, and wheeling.

2. **Part A:** Choice A is correct. These characters are not given names; instead, they are identified by their jobs.

   Part B: Choice B is correct. Those characters seem to be everywhere, directing everything, causing trouble to the workers.

3. **Part A:** Choice C is correct. The Driver and Overseer want the baby to be quiet, but they hit the child, which is counterproductive.

   Part B: Choice A is correct. Three similes are used in succession: "she rose just as free as a bird," "light as a feather," and "flew like an eagle."

4. **Part A:** Choice A is correct. The Overseer has been empowered by man; the author contrasts this depiction by suggesting that Toby has been empowered by a deity.

   Part B: Choice B is correct. How else would we have a story? The author infers that this was the reason in the last paragraph.

5. **Part A:** Choice C is correct. He asserts in the first paragraph that the "dashing surf" would violently rock the ship, breaking people's limbs and sometimes killing him. He also discusses the change in climate from temperate and hot. Although he does discuss being robbed by two sailors (B), this does not happen "day by day;" it has only happened once.

   Part B: Statement 2 directly supports choice C in Part A.

6. **Part A:** Claim 1 is the only claim supported in the text. Claim two is not necessarily true. While it could be said that slaves were fed poorly, it was not necessarily true that they never learned a trade. Claim 3 is clearly not true as Equiano discusses a couple of his masters who were kind to him and who fed him well.

   Part B: Statements 1, 5, and 8 support claim 1. In these statements, Equiano explains that he worked hard, he knew that there were men who would treat him poorly, and the conditions in which he worked were not always safe.

7. **Part A:** Equiano makes several references to the opinion that his owners had of him. Therefore, he explains that a previous master said he was a good worker. This is choice D.

   Part B: Choice A is the direct quote from the passage.

8. **Part A:** The job of ellipses is to shorten longer pieces of text; this is choice B.

   Part B: In the beginning of the selection, Equiano personifies his fate and provides a capital letter. At the end of the selection, he discusses his own fate. This is explained in choice C.

9. **Part A:** Rough seas are in both texts. This is choice B.

   Part B: Choice A is the only choice that is accurate.

10. The purpose of this story was to provide hope of a way out of a terrible situation. The audience for "The People Could Fly" is African-Americans who might be enslaved; the justification of these selections can be found in the conclusion of the tale; it implies that although they were enslaved, they were left behind to tell the story of an escape to freedom.

    The purpose of this selection of Equiano's narrative was to explain how slaves were bought and sold as there were several mentions of this practice (justification). It appears that Equiano's audience was Americans who wanted to end slavery. Equiano realized that people could not put an end to a practice that they did not understand.

Part Two

Reading Comprehension

70 minutes

Directions: Walt Whitman is one of America's most celebrated poets. During the Civil War, Whitman moved to Washington, D.C., to take care of his brother who was injured in battle. While he lived in Washington, D.C., he occasionally saw President Lincoln.

Today, you will read about Whitman's reaction to Lincoln's assassination by reading an excerpt from Whitman's diary and one of Whitman's poems. As you read, you will respond to questions about each text. The last two questions will ask you about both texts.

Excerpt from *The Lincoln Anthology: Great Writers on His Legacy from 1860 to Now* (Library of America, 2009), edited by Harold Holzer, pp. 249–251 © 2009 Literary Classics of the U.S., Inc. http://www.loa.org/images/pdf/Whitman_on_Lincoln.pdf

Whitman on Lincoln

Although Whitman almost certainly only imagined Lincoln acknowledging the poet's occasional sightings of him on the streets of Washington, it is clear from his recollections that he treasured such "encounters" and experienced a genuine thrill in Lincoln's presence. In prose as well as verse, Whitman remembered and celebrated Lincoln as the supreme embodiment of American democracy and "Nationality." The first selection printed here dates from the summer of 1863.

August 12th.—I see the President almost every day, as I happen to live where he passes to or from his lodgings out of town. He never sleeps at the White House during the hot season, but has quarters at a healthy location some three miles north of the city, the Soldiers' home, a United States military establishment. I saw him this morning about half-past eight coming in to business, riding on Vermont avenue, near L street. He always has a company of twenty-five or thirty cavalry, with sabres drawn and held upright over their shoulders. They say this guard was against his personal wish, but he let his counselors have their way. The party makes no great show in uniform or horses. Mr. Lincoln on the saddle generally rides a good-sized, easy-going gray horse, is dress'd in plain black, somewhat rusty and dusty, wears a black stiff hat, and looks about as ordinary in attire, as the commonest man. A lieutenant, with yellow straps, rides at his left, and following behind, two by two, come the cavalry men, in their yellow-striped jackets. They are generally going at a slow trot, as that is the pace set them by the one they wait upon. The sabres and accoutrements clank, and the entirely un-ornamental cortége as it trots towards Lafayette square arouses no sensation, only some curious stranger stops and gazes. I see very plainly Abraham Lincoln's dark brown face, with the deep-cut lines, the eyes, always to me with a deep latent sadness in the expression. We have got so that we exchange bows, and very cordial ones. Sometimes the President goes and comes in an open barouche. The cavalry always accompany him, with drawn sabres. Often I notice as he goes out evenings—and sometimes in the morning, when he returns early— he turns off and halts at the large and handsome residence of the Secretary of War, on K street, and holds conference there. If in his barouche, I can see from my window he does not alight, but sits in his vehicle, and Mr. Stanton comes out to attend him. Sometimes one of his sons, a boy of ten or twelve, accompanies him, riding at his right on a pony. Earlier in the summer I occasionally saw the President and his wife, toward the latter part of the afternoon, out in a barouche, on a pleasure ride through the city. Mrs. Lincoln was dress'd in complete black, with a long crape veil. The equipage is of the plainest kind, only two horses, and they nothing extra. They pass'd me once very close, and I saw the President in the face fully, as they were moving slowly, and his look, though abstracted, happened to be directed steadily in my eye. He bow'd and smiled, but far beneath his smile I noticed well the expression I have alluded to. None of the artists or pictures has caught the deep, though subtle and indirect expression of this man's face. There is something else there. One of the great portrait painters of two or three centuries ago is needed.

Death of President Lincoln

<u>April 16, '65.</u>—I find in my notes of the time, this passage on the death of Abraham Lincoln: He leaves for America's history and biography, so far, not only its most dramatic reminiscence —he leaves, in my opinion, the greatest, best, most characteristic, artistic, moral personality. Not but that he had faults, and show'd them in the Presidency; but honesty, goodness, shrewdness, conscience, and (a new virtue, unknown to other lands, and hardly yet really known here, but the foundation and tie of all, as the future will grandly develop,) Unionism, in its truest and amplest sense, form'd the hard-pan of his character. These he seal'd with his life. The tragic splendor of his death, purging, illuminating all, throws round his form, his head, an aureole that will remain and will grow brighter through time, while history lives, and love of country lasts. By many has this Union been help'd; but if

one name, one man, must be pick'd out, he, most of all, is the conservator of it, to the future. He was assassinated—but the Union is not assassinated! One falls, and another falls. The soldier drops, sinks like a wave—but the ranks of the ocean eternally press on. Death does its work, obliterates a hundred, a thousand—President, general, captain, private—but the Nation is immortal.

Question One

Part A

Whitman's description of Lincoln leads the reader to believe that Lincoln is what kind of man?

- ○ A. important
- ○ B. ordinary
- ○ C. caring
- ○ D. neglectful

Part B

What evidence from the text supports your reasoning for the Part A?
Select all that apply.

1	"He never sleeps at the White House during the hot season, but has quarters at a healthy location some three miles north of the city,...."
2	"He bow'd and smiled, but far beneath his smile I noticed well the expression I have alluded to."
3	"The equipage is of the plainest kind, only two horses, and they nothing extra."
4	"He always has a company of twenty-five or thirty cavalry, with sabres drawn and held upright over their shoulders."
5	"If in his barouche, I can see from my window he does not alight, but sits in his vehicle, and Mr. Stanton comes out to attend him."
6	"Mr. Lincoln on the saddle generally rides a good-sized, easy-going gray horse, is dress'd in plain black, somewhat rusty and dusty, wears a black stiff hat...."

Question Two

Part A

Why do the horses move at a slow trot?

- ○ A. They are on parade.
- ○ B. They moved slowly because there were so many military men to protect Lincoln.
- ○ C. They had no where in particular to go.
- ○ D. They move at the speed Lincoln sets.

Part B

What evidence from the text supports your answer for Part A?

- ○ A. "They pass'd me once very close, and I saw the President in the face fully, as they were moving slowly,..."
- ○ B. "as that is the pace set them by the one they wait upon."
- ○ C. "They say this guard was against his personal wish, but he let his counselors have their way."
- ○ D. "The cavalry always accompany him, with drawn sabres."

Question Three

Part A

Whitman remarks,

"They pass'd me once very close, and I saw the President in the face fully, as they were moving slowly, and his look, though abstracted, happened to be directed steadily in my eye. He bow'd and smiled, but far beneath his smile I noticed well the expression I have alluded to. None of the artists or pictures has caught the deep, though subtle and indirect expression of this man's face. There is something else there. One of the great portrait painters of two or three centuries ago is needed."

What does he expect a great portrait painter to capture that a photograph cannot?

- ○ A. The smile upon Lincoln's face
- ○ B. The full height of Lincoln's body
- ○ C. The thoughtful look in Lincoln's demeanor
- ○ D. The sharp angles in Lincoln's face

Part B
In this remark,

> "They pass'd me once very close, and I saw the President in the face fully, as they were moving slowly, and his look, though abstracted, happened to be directed steadily in my eye. He bow'd and smiled, but far beneath his smile I noticed well the expression I have alluded to. None of the artists or pictures has caught the deep, though subtle and indirect expression of this man's face. There is something else there. One of the great portrait painters of two or three centuries ago is needed."

Whitman observes that the President is *abstracted*. In this context, what does *abstracted* mean?

- ○ A. Focused on a particular image
- ○ B. Lost in thought
- ○ C. Older than it appears
- ○ D. Shortened from its original length

Question Four

Part A
Whitman frequently lists items in his poetry and prose. From the choices below, select the examples that demonstrate how Whitman incorporates this technique in his writing.

1	"Not but that he had faults, and show'd them in the Presidency; but honesty, goodness, shrewdness, conscience, and (a new virtue, unknown to other lands, and hardly yet really known here, but the foundation and tie of all, as the future will grandly develop,) Unionism, in its truest and amplest sense, form'd the hard-pan of his character."
2	"Earlier in the summer I occasionally saw the President and his wife, toward the latter part of the afternoon, out in a barouche, on a pleasure ride through the city."
3	"I find in my notes of the time, this passage on the death of Abraham Lincoln:..."
4	"Death does its work, obliterates a hundred, a thousand—President, general, captain, private—but the Nation is immortal."
5	"I see very plainly Abraham Lincoln's dark brown face, with the deep-cut lines, the eyes, always to me with a deep latent sadness in the expression"

Part B

What is the effect of employing this literary device into prose?

- ○ A. It provides the reader with a sense that Whitman was very passionate about how important he believed Lincoln was.
- ○ B. It demonstrates that Whitman was very objective in his analysis of Lincoln's death.
- ○ C. It shows that events in history will live on forever as long as they are frequently discussed.
- ○ D. It develops the foundation for a speech.

Question Five

Part A

Whitman claims that Lincoln demonstrated *Unionism*. Which of the following best explains how Whitman would define the term *Unionism*?

- ○ A. the idea of bringing North America into one large country
- ○ B. the spirit of cooperation with all Americans
- ○ C. the demonstration of power against the South
- ○ D. the connection that was forged between the East Coast and the newer states

Part B

Why does Whitman believe that Unionism is a new characteristic of man?

- ○ A. Not many men can cooperate with others.
- ○ B. There are few instances in history where one part of a large country forges connections with another part of the country.
- ○ C. The concept of a nation united by people was relatively new in Whitman's time.
- ○ D. Although many nations have experienced Civil Wars, they have not been able to stay together as the United States was able to do.

Question Six

What predictions does Whitman make about the death of Lincoln?

Select all that apply.

1	Even though Lincoln was a great president, not many people will care about him in the future.
2	Although Lincoln died, the goals that Lincoln had set forth have been accomplished and will not be undone.
3	Lincoln is so important that towns will be named and cities will be erected in his honor.
4	As time goes on, his legacy will become more important and his time in office will appear to have a "glow" about it.
5	The South will leave the Union again because Lincoln is not there to hold the country together.
6	There will be few leaders, if any, who will ever live up to Lincoln's legacy.

Whitman, Walt. "O Captain! My Captain!" *Leaves of Grass*. Oxford: Oxford University Press, 1990. (1865)

O Captain! My Captain!

Walt Whitman

O Captain! my Captain! our fearful trip is done;

The ship has weather'd every rack, the prize we sought is won;

The port is near, the bells I hear, the people all exulting,

While follow eyes the steady keel, the vessel grim and daring:

But O heart! heart! heart!

O the bleeding drops of red,

Where on the deck my Captain lies,

Fallen cold and dead.

O Captain! my Captain! rise up and hear the bells;

Rise up—for you the flag is flung—for you the bugle trills;

For you bouquets and ribbon'd wreaths—for you the shores a-crowding;

For you they call, the swaying mass, their eager faces turning;

Here Captain! dear father!

This arm beneath your head;

It is some dream that on the deck,

You've fallen cold and dead.

My Captain does not answer, his lips are pale and still;

My father does not feel my arm, he has no pulse nor will;

The ship is anchor'd safe and sound, its voyage closed and done;

From fearful trip, the victor ship, comes in with object won;

Exult, O shores, and ring, O bells!

But I, with mournful tread,

Walk the deck my Captain lies,

Fallen cold and dead.

Question Seven

Part A

What is the extended metaphor established the first verse?

- ○ A. The ship is a metaphor for the United States.
- ○ B. The port is a metaphor for the Confederacy.
- ○ C. The heart is a metaphor for the brothers who fought in the war.
- ○ D. The bell is a metaphor for the sound of gunfire.

Part B

What is an example of the metaphor being continued through the poem?

- ○ A. "My Captain does not answer, his lips are pale and still;\My father does not feel my arm, he has no pulse nor will;"
- ○ B. "….For you the bugle trills;\For you bouquets and ribbon'd wreaths—for you the shores a-crowding;"
- ○ C. "The ship is anchor'd safe and sound, its voyage closed and done; \From fearful trip, the victor ship, comes in with object won;"
- ○ D. "For you they call, the swaying mass, their eager faces turning;\Here Captain! dear father!"

Question Eight

Part A

What irony is present in the poem?

- ○ A. The ship has not completed its voyage, but people are still cheering for its return.
- ○ B. The crowd is cheering for the captain even though he sinks the ship.
- ○ C. The captain has died just as the ship has arrived in the port.
- ○ D. The ship was not built in the United States, but Americans think that it was.

Part B

Why does Whitman use the word *father* in the poem?

- ○ A. As the president, Lincoln is the father to the country.
- ○ B. It is important for children to know who their fathers are.
- ○ C. Whitman is asking his father why Lincoln has died.
- ○ D. The captain has a lot of children.

Question Nine

Part A

Whitman says in the first stanza that people are *exulting*; what does the word *exulting* mean?

○ A. cheering
○ B. booing
○ C. rioting
○ D. crying

Part B

How does Whitman demonstrate how the people feel about the captain?

○ A. He creates the image of people screaming.
○ B. He repeats the phrase, "O, Captain!" throughout the text.
○ C. He tells the people to cheer as the boat arrives into the port.
○ D. He explains to the captain's dead body that the people are cheering for him.

Question Ten

How does Whitman emphasize the gravity of Lincoln's death? Drag and drop the rhetorical strategies that are employed in the poem and in the prose.

1	repetition of a word or phrase
2	creating the image of a halo around Lincoln's body
3	comparing Lincoln's death to the death of George Washington
4	a catalogue of descriptive words
5	imagery of a funeral
6	a lengthy description of the strategic choices that Lincoln made for the army

Strategy Used in the Poem	Strategy Used in the Prose

Answers

Question	Part A	Part B
1	B	3, 6
2	D	B
3	C	B
4	1, 4	A
5	B	C
6	2, 4	
7	A	C
8	C	A
9	A	D
10	Poem: 1, 5	Prose: 2, 4

Answers Explained

1. **Part A:** Choice B states that Lincoln was depicted as an ordinary man.

   Part B: The third quote states that the procession was "plain." The six quote uses the word "plain" and describes what might have been a regular man's procession as items were "somewhat rusty and dusty," not immaculately clean.

2. **Part A:** Choice D is correct; this was the speed that Lincoln set.

   Part B: The evidence that supports choice D in Part A is "the pace set by the one they wait upon." The one the horses waited upon was Lincoln.

3. **Part A:** Choice C is correct. The passage is primarily focused upon how it might be possible to capture the process of Lincoln thinking.

   Part B: Because the passage discusses thought, it is reasonable to conclude that the word *abstracted* to mean lost in thought. This is choice B.

4. **Part A:** The two choices that have lists in them are choices 1 and 4.

   Part B: The lists that Whitman creates demonstrate his enthusiasm for Lincoln. This is best expressed in choice A.

5. **Part A:** Remember that Whitman and Lincoln lived during the time of the Civil War. Unionists wanted the country to remain as one. Therefore, the best response is choice B.

   Part B: For the same reason as explained above, choice C is the best response.

6. The answers are statements 2 and 4. Statement 2 was, "Although Lincoln died, the goals that Lincoln had set forth have been accomplished and will not be undone." Lincoln's goal was to maintain the Union. He accomplished this; Whitman notes that although Lincoln was assassinated, the union (his accomplishment) was not killed. Whitman's last line is, "the Nation is immortal."

   Statement 4 was "As time goes on, his legacy will become more important and his time in office will appear to have a 'glow' about it." This is a rewording from this part of the text, "The tragic splendor of his death, purging, illuminating all, throws round his form, his head, an aureole that will remain and will grow brighter through time, while history lives, and love of country lasts."

7. **Part A:** Whitman makes a direct comparison between the ship and the United States; this is choice A.

   Part B: In choice C, Whitman says that the trip is over and the "object won." The trip is the war; the object won is the union.

8. **Part A:** Choice C is correct. Just as the war ended, Lincoln was assassinated. This is depicted in the poem as the captain dying just as the ship comes to the port.

   Part B: The answer is choice A; the president is the "father" of the country.

9. **Part A:** The answer is choice A; the word *exult* means to cheer.

   Part B: Choice D is correct; the poet is addressing the dead body of the captain. He tells it that people are cheering for the man who inhabited the body.

10. Statement 1: Repetition of the words "O Captain, my captain" and "fallen cold and dead" are used in the poem.

    Statement 2: Whitman says that Lincoln has an aura about him in the description of his death in the prose (essay).

    Statement 3: No comparison is made between Lincoln and Washington.

Statement 4: As you might recall from question 4, the catalogue, or list, is in the prose.

Statement 5: The funeral images are in the poem (vessel grim, wreaths, bugle trills).

Statement 6: There are no descriptions in either poem or prose about Lincoln's military strategy.

Analytic Writing: Analytic writing uses evidence from the text to convey ideas and arguments. This type of test differs from other tests that ask students to write without relation to anything they have read. It links writing to reading.

Anchor Text: The anchor text is the first text students read; it introduces the bigger topic. Students will also read the other texts that follow the anchor text that have the same topic or theme.

Claim: PARCC breaks down the overall score into master claims and subclaims, which show student results in multiple Common Core categories. Claim is also the main point the essay makes. The Common Core uses the term claim. Claim replaces the term thesis statements.

Common Core: Officially, it is the Common Core State Standards, but it is called the Common Core for short. The Common Core attempts to create a unified set of standards in English Language Arts and in Math for each grade level, no matter what state the students resides.

Complexity: Different questions have different levels of complexity, or cognitive levels that students need to answer a particular question.

Device: A device is a computer, laptop, or tablet that a student uses in school and/or uses to take the PARCC.

Diagnostic Assessment: In addition to the summative PBA and EOY, PARCC will also offer a Diagnostic Assessment (starting in the 2015–16 school year) and a Mid-Year Assessment (starting in the 2014–15 school year). These tests do not count toward students' PARCC scores. Instead, they are to help students get used to the test and to help guide instruction for teachers, who will see students' strengths and weaknesses.

EBSR: The Evidence-Based Selected Response is one of the three kinds of items on the PBA and EOY. It will measure students' reading proficiency at grade-level PARCC standards. The EBSR is really two questions. The first is like a standard reading comprehension question, but the second is different from most standardized test questions. The second question asks the student for the textual evidence that proves the first question. It is part of what makes PARCC a "deeper" test.

ECD: PARCC uses Evidence-Centered Design to develop the test. Each task on the test is designed to follow first a claim about what students can do and then evidence that would prove those claims.

Embedded Support: PARCC will use embedded support to help on the test. One such embedded support tool will be a highlighter.

ELA: ELA is short for English Language Arts. Both terms are used interchangeably to describe students' language courses.

EOY: The EOY is the End-of-Year assessment. The EOY is given about 90 percent of the way through the school year. It has two parts, and both are reading only. There are no writing tasks on the EOY.

Item: An Item is a question or task on the test.

Mid-Year Assessment: Like the Diagnostic Assessment (starting in the 2015–16 school year), PARCC will offer a Mid-Year Assessment (starting in the 2014–15 school year). Again, these tests do not count toward students' PARCC scores. Instead, they are to help students get used to the test and to help guide instruction for teachers, who will see students' strengths and weaknesses.

Non-Summative Assessments: Non-Summative Assessments are designed to help students get used to the Summative Assessment and to show teachers where students need more work or help. They do not count toward the Scale Score. PARCC's Non-Summative Assessments are the Diagnostic Assessment and Mid-Year Assessment.

PARCC: The full name for PARCC is the Partnership for Assessment of Readiness for College and Careers. It is designed to coincide with Common Core, and it is designed to replace all the individual state tests.

PBA: The PBA is the Performance-Based Assessment. It is given about 75 percent of the way through the school year. It has three parts: a Literary Analysis Task, a Narrative Writing Task, and a Research Simulation Task. There are both reading and writing questions on the PBA.

PCR: As part of each section of the PBA, students are asked to create a Prose Constructed Response. Generally, it is an essay or story (depending on the prompt) based on the text for the PBA.

PLD: To grade the PARCC writing prompts, Performance Level Descriptors are used. The writing is scored on a holistic scale (1–5 for grade 8) on a combination of text complexity, range of accuracy, and quality of evidence.

Scale Score: The Scale Score is the overall test score for the PARCC. It is based on Performance Level Descriptors, and it shows where students are according to the Common Core standards for their grade level.

Speaking and Listening Assessments: The Common Core standards for ELA state that students must be able to communicate orally and listen to others. PARCC will have a non-summative component for Speaking and Listening (it will not count toward the Scale Score).

Summative Assessments: Summative Assessments are given at the end of instruction and count toward the Scale Score. PARCC's Summative Assessments are the PBA and the EOY. Its Non-Summative Assessments are the Diagnostic Assessment and Mid-Year Assessment.

Task: A task is group of items based on a text. These items can include comprehension, evidence, and vocabulary questions in the PBA and EOY, and they can also include a written Prose Constructed Response in the PBA.

TECR: The Technology-Enhanced Constructed Response is like the EBSR in that it is two questions, the first asking a reading comprehension question. In a TECR second question, students are asked to go back to the test and highlight and paste evidence for the first question into the answer box. Like the EBSR, it not only asks the student a comprehension question but also asks the student to find the evidence that proves it in the text.

TEIs: PARCC will use Technology-Enhanced Items like videos. This is one of the new ways PARCC will be different from the standard pencil-and-paper tests it will replace.

Test Form: The Test Form is the collection of items and tasks that together make the full assessment.

Vertical Scale: PARCC will use a vertical scale to show student growth and progress from grade level to grade level. Since PARCC will be given every year, it will show students' growth over time.

Condensed Scoring Rubric

Prose Constructed Response Items: Grade 8

Construct Measured	
Reading Comprehension of Key Ideas and Details	
Score Point 4	The student response provides an accurate analysis of what the text says explicitly and inferentially and cites convincing textual evidence to support the analysis, showing full comprehension of complex ideas expressed in the text(s).
Score Point 3	The student response provides a mostly accurate analysis of what the text says explicitly and inferentially and cites textual evidence to support the analysis, showing extensive comprehension of ideas expressed in the text(s).
Score Point 2	The student response provides a generally accurate analysis of what the text says explicitly or inferentially and cited textual evidence, shows a basic comprehension of ideas expressed in the text(s).
Score Point 1	The student response provides a minimally accurate analysis of what the text says and cited textual evidence, shows limited comprehension of ideas expressed in the text(s).
Score Point 0	The student response provides an inaccurate analysis or no analysis of the text, showing little to no comprehension of ideas expressed in the text(s).

*Notes The type of textual evidence required is grade and prompt specific and included in the scoring guide.

Construct Measured	
Writing	
Written Expression	
Score Point 4	—The student response addresses the prompt and provides effective and comprehensive development of the claim, topic and/or narrative elements by using clear and convincing reasoning, details, text-based evidence, and/or description; the development is consistently appropriate to the task, purpose, and audience. —The student response demonstrates purposeful coherence, clarity, and cohesion and includes a strong introduction, conclusion, and a logical, well-executed progression of ideas, making it easy to follow the writer's progression of ideas. —The student response establishes and maintains an effective style, while attending to the norms and conventions of the discipline. The response uses precise language consistently, including descriptive words and phrases, sensory details, linking and transitional words, words to indicate tone, and/or domain-specific vocabulary.
Score Point 3	—The student response addresses the prompt and provides effective development of the claim, topic and/or narrative elements by using clear reasoning, details, text-based evidence, and/or description; the development is largely appropriate to the task, purpose, and audience. —The student response demonstrates a great deal of coherence, clarity, and cohesion, and includes an introduction, conclusion, and a logical progression of ideas, making it fairly easy to follow the writer's progression of ideas. —The student response establishes and maintains an effective style, while attending to the norms and conventions of the discipline. The response uses mostly precise language, including descriptive words and phrases, sensory details, linking and transitional words, words to indicate tone, and/or domain-specific vocabulary.

Score Point 2	—The student response addresses the prompt and provides some development of the claim, topic and/or narrative elements by using some reasoning, details, text-based evidence, and/or description; the development is somewhat appropriate to the task, purpose, and audience. —The student response demonstrates some coherence, clarity, and/or cohesion, and includes an introduction, conclusion, and logically grouped ideas, making the writer's progression of ideas usually discernible but not obvious. —The student response establishes and maintains a mostly effective style, while attending to the norms and conventions of the discipline. The response uses some precise language, including descriptive words and phrases, sensory details, linking and transitional words, words to indicate tone and/or domain-specific vocabulary.
Score Point 1	—The student response addresses the prompt and develops the claim, topic and/or narrative elements minimally by using limited reasoning, details, text-based evidence and/or description; the development is limited in its appropriateness to the task, purpose, and/or audience. —The student response demonstrates limited coherence, clarity, and/or cohesion, making the writer's progression of ideas somewhat unclear. —The student response has a style that has limited effectiveness, with limited awareness of the norms of the discipline. The response includes limited descriptions, sensory details, linking or transitional words, words to indicate tone, or domain-specific vocabulary.
Score Point 0	—The student response is underdeveloped and therefore inappropriate to the task, purpose, and/or audience. —The student response demonstrates a lack of coherence, clarity and cohesion. —The student response has an inappropriate style. The student writing shows little to no awareness of the norms of the discipline. The response includes little to no precise language.

Construct Measured	
Writing Knowledge of Language and Conventions	
Score Point 4	The student response demonstrates command of the conventions of standard English consistent with effectively edited writing. Though there may be a few minor errors in grammar and usage, meaning is clear throughout the response.
Score Point 3	The student response demonstrates command of the conventions of standard English consistent with edited writing. There may be a few distracting errors in grammar and usage, but meaning is clear.
Score Point 2	The student response demonstrates inconsistent command of the conventions of standard English. There are a few patterns of errors in grammar and usage that may occasionally impede understanding.
Score Point 1	The student response demonstrates limited command of the conventions of standard English. There are multiple errors in grammar and usage demonstrating minimal control over language. There are multiple distracting errors in grammar and usage that sometimes impede understanding.
Score Point 0	The student response demonstrates little to no command of the conventions of standard English. There are frequent and varied errors in grammar and usage, demonstrating little or no control over language. There are frequent distracting errors in grammar and usage that often impede understanding.

Index

A

Anecdote, 96

B

Body paragraphs, 95–96, 103–105

C

Charts, 61, 84
Citations, 77
Common Core State Standards, 1
Comparison and contrast, 67, 74–75
Complex sentences, 9
Conclusion, of essay, 96–97, 105
Connotation, 15

D

Direct characterization, 9
Draft, 55

E

End-of-Year assessment
    description of, 5
    reading comprehension practice,
        161–190
    sample, 161–190
Essay
    body paragraphs of, 95–96, 103–105
    conclusion of, 96–97, 105
    introduction of, 96–97, 103
    thesis of, 92–94
Essay question, 89
Essay writing
    description of, 79–80
    example of, 103–105, 120–124,
        132–136, 144–148
    planning of, 90–92

Evidence, 77
Evidence-based constructed response
    question, 1–2

F

Figurative language, 9, 14

G

Graphic organizer, 64

I

Ideas, organizing of, 76
Indirect characterization, 9
Introduction, of essay, 96–97, 103

L

Literary analysis task
    comparison and contrast, 67, 74–75
    essay writing, 79–80
    example of, 4, 125–136
    note taking, 67–73
    outline, 75–78
    time allowed for, 67
Logic, 90

M

Main idea questions, 15–17, 25–31
Mini research paper, 83–84
Multiple-choice questions, 12–14

N

Narrative writing task
    charts, 61
    completing a story, 52–58
    draft, 55

explanatory, 49
graphic organizer, 64
historical account, 58–62
outline used in, 54–55
prompt, 49–50
samples, 52–65, 137–148
scientific process, 63–65
speculative, 49–51
summary of, 66
time allowed for, 49
National Governors Association, 1
Note taking, 67–73

O

Outline
literary analysis task use of, 75–78
narrative writing task use of, 54–55

P

PARCC
administration of, 1–4
description of, 1
parts of, 4–5
scoring of, 5–6, 195–198
summary of, 6
timing of, 4–5
two-part questions on, 14
Performance-based assessment
parts of, 5
sample, 107–160
Performance level descriptor, 5–6
Poems, 10–11
Prompt, 49–50
Prose constructed response questions
preparation for, 66
types of, 3

R

Reading
main idea questions, 15–17, 25–31
multiple-choice questions, 12–14

poems, 10–11
practice, 19–47, 161–190
selections for, 7–11
summarizing questions, 15–17
supporting details questions, 18–19, 32
vocabulary questions, 14–15, 22–25
Reading the directions, 85–88
Research paper, 83–84
Research simulation task
body paragraphs of essay, 92–94, 103–105
essay writing, 90–92
example of, 97–105
mini research paper, 83–84
reading the directions, 85–88
reading the essay question, 89
sample, 107–119
summary of, 106
thesis of essay, 92–94
time allowed for, 84

S

Sandburg, Carl, 10
Scoring rubric, 195–198
Summarizing questions, 15–17
Supporting details questions, 18–19, 32

T

T-chart, 67–68, 81
Technology-enhanced constructed response question, 2–3
TestNav, 1
Thesis, 92–94

V

Venn diagram, 67
Vocabulary questions, 14–15, 22–25

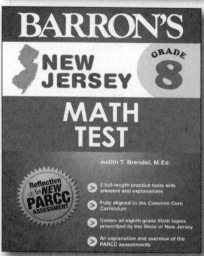

Really. This isn't going to hurt at all . . .

Learning won't hurt when middle school and high school students open any *Painless* title. These books transform subjects into fun—emphasizing a touch of humor and entertaining brain-tickler puzzles that are fun to solve.

Extra bonus—each title followed by (*) comes with a FREE app!
Download a fun-to-play arcade game to your iPhone, iTouch, iPad, or Android™ device. The games reinforce the study material in each book and provide hours of extra fun.

Each book: Paperback

Painless Algebra, 3rd Ed.*
Lynette Long, Ph.D.
ISBN 978-0-7641-4715-9, $9.99, *Can$11.99*

Painless American Government
Jeffrey Strausser
ISBN 978-0-7641-2601-7, $9.99, *Can$11.99*

Painless American History, 2nd Ed.
Curt Lader
ISBN 978-0-7641-4231-4, $9.99, *Can$11.99*

Painless Chemistry*
Loris Chen
ISBN 978-0-7641-4602-2, $9.99, *Can$11.99*

Painless Earth Science*
Edward J. Denecke, Jr.
ISBN 978-0-7641-4601-5, $9.99, *Can$11.99*

Painless English for Speakers of Other Languages, 2nd Ed.*
Jeffrey Strausser and José Paniza
ISBN 978-1-4380-0002-2, $9.99, *Can$11.50*

Painless Fractions, 3rd Ed.*
Alyece Cummings, M.A.
ISBN 978-1-4380-0000-8, $9.99, *Can$11.50*

Painless French, 2nd Ed.*
Carol Chaitkin, M.S., and Lynn Gore, M.A.
ISBN 978-0-7641-4762-3, $9.99, *Can$11.50*

Painless Geometry, 2nd Ed.
Lynette Long, Ph.D.
ISBN 978-0-7641-4230-7, $9.99, *Can$11.99*

Painless Grammar, 3rd Ed.*
Rebecca S. Elliott, Ph.D.
ISBN 978-0-7641-4712-8, $9.99, *Can$11.99*

Painless Italian, 2nd Ed.*
Marcel Danesi, Ph.D.
ISBN 978-0-7641-4761-6, $9.99, *Can$11.50*

Painless Math Word Problems, 2nd Ed.
Marcie Abramson, B.S., Ed.M.
ISBN 978-0-7641-4335-9, $9.99, *Can$11.99*

Painless Poetry, 2nd Ed.
Mary Elizabeth
ISBN 978-0-7641-4591-9, $9.99, *Can$11.99*

Painless Pre-Algebra
Amy Stahl
ISBN 978-0-7641-4588-9, $9.99, *Can$11.99*

Painless Reading Comprehension, 2nd Ed.*
Darolyn E. Jones, Ed.D.
ISBN 978-0-7641-4763-0, $9.99, *Can$11.50*

Painless Spanish, 2nd Ed.*
Carlos B. Vega
ISBN 978-0-7641-4711-1, $9.99, *Can$11.99*

Painless Speaking, 2nd Ed.*
Mary Elizabeth
ISBN 978-1-4380-0003-9, $9.99, *Can$11.50*

Painless Spelling, 3rd Ed.*
Mary Elizabeth
ISBN 978-0-7641-4713-5, $9.99, *Can$11.99*

Painless Study Techniques
Michael Greenberg
ISBN 978-0-7641-4059-4, $9.99, *Can$11.99*

Painless Vocabulary, 2nd Ed.*
Michael Greenberg
ISBN 978-0-7641-4714-2, $9.99, *Can$11.99*

Painless Writing, 2nd Ed.
Jeffrey Strausser
ISBN 978-0-7641-4234-5, $9.99, *Can$11.99*

Prices subject to change without notice.

Available at your local book store
or visit **www.barronseduc.com**

(#79) R4/14

Barron's Educational Series, Inc.
250 Wireless Blvd.
Hauppauge, N.Y. 11788
Order toll-free:
1-800-645-3476